# On the Trail
# of God

*Books by William Proctor*

On the Trail of God
Survival on the Campus: A Handbook for Christian Students
Help Wanted: Faith Required
The Commune Kidnapping

*By Priscilla and William Proctor*

Women in the Pulpit

*By Alphonse Calabrese and William Proctor*

RX: The Christian Love Treatment

# On the Trail
# of God

*by William Proctor*

DOUBLEDAY & COMPANY, INC.
GARDEN CITY, NEW YORK
1977

Lines from the song "Miracles" by Noel Paul Stookey courtesy of Noel
Paul Stookey Domain Fund

Library of Congress Cataloging in Publication Data

Proctor, William.
On the trail of God.

1. Converts—United States—Biography.   I. Title.
BV4930.P23     248'.2'0924 [B]
ISBN 0-385-11680-2
Library of Congress Catalog Card Number 76–42385

*to Pam*

# Contents

# A Personal Note

## WILLIAM PROCTOR

It's hard to find a Southern Baptist agnostic in Dallas, Texas. But when I was about seventeen years old, I was well on my way toward becoming just such a curious phenomenon. The summer before my senior year in high school, I had traveled to Europe on a foreign exchange student program, and my fragile beliefs had been profoundly shaken. My Evangelical Christian upbringing had failed to prepare me for the questions that sophisticated students from around the country raised:

"Why do you believe Jesus Christ is the Son of God?"

"Don't you realize there are good psychological explanations for so-called spiritual experiences?"

"How do you even know God exists?"

I tried to respond intelligently to their questions, but I failed because my own spiritual life was quite limited. If I had been honest, my answers to all their queries would have been, "I really don't know." My faith—if you can call it that—was mostly a cultural thing, shaped by the church, my family, and a few authentic Christians who had chanced across my path. I prayed occasionally. I gave lip service to traditional Christian doctrines. But my religion was not really my own; God was not really at the center of my life.

The challenges hurled at me on that cruise seemed to wake me up, spiritually speaking. It seemed as though I had been dozing complacently, unaware of the variety of spiritual possibilities that confront the person who has embarked on a serious search for ultimate meaning. At the sound of these discordant, skeptical student voices, I opened my eyes and was immediately immobilized by confusion. Which direction should I take? What world view should I choose? How could I pick "God's way," since I doubted deep inside that there was any God at all?

My parents, my pastor, and a few other older authority figures heard me out and tried to help. Somehow, I didn't have ears to hear or the eyes to see what they were trying to communicate. But one piece of Scriptural advice from my parents stuck with me. They reminded me of Jesus' words in Luke 11:9: "Ask, and it will be given you; seek, and you will find; knock, and it will be opened to you." So I kept seeking, kept banging on the door to heaven, kept asking God to reveal Himself.

For a while—months, in fact—my prayers seemed to echo meaninglessly in a vacuum. I sensed I was probably talking to myself. Then God responded. As I lay in bed one night, my thoughts wandered in frustration back to Him. "I've got to know! If you're out there, God, show me!"

Suddenly, a cold sweat covered my body, and an inexplicable awe gripped me. Something from outside myself seemed to grasp my mind, and my thoughts were directed toward God and a consciousness of His presence. For a few moments, I knew beyond any shadow of doubt that God was there. There was no question that He existed and that Jesus Christ, His Son, had suffered the penalty for my sins, my disobedience to God, on the cross. Overcome by God's love for me, I surrendered to a wave of emotion, and tears welled up in my eyes. My preliminary search for God was over. But a long, exciting, and sometimes nerve-racking journey through life with Him was only beginning.

I haven't told many people about this experience because I haven't always known exactly how to interpret it. I now regard that moment as a kind of conversion, a turning from cultural Christianity toward an inner, vital, self-starting faith. I believe that the Holy Spirit—God's constantly present, empowering Personal Presence with us—responded to my serious seeking, as Jesus had promised. The Spirit actually dwelled inside me, and in effect said through my mind, "Okay, now you know. Christ left Me here just as He said He would (John 15:26). From here on, it's up to you to keep Me inside you; to follow My leading; to be obedient when I prod you in this direction or that."

Of course, I haven't always been obedient to God's inner voice. And the less obedient I am, the more the old doubts about His power and very existence seem to grip me. But when I put God first, when I submit my will to Him, He has been faithful to reveal His wishes to me. Occasionally His communications have been extraordinary: I may get a definite impression of His comforting presence as I did that night in Dallas, with definite thought direction and even a physical tingling. These experiences may be followed by a definite impression of something God wants me to do. More often, He speaks through more ordinary channels, including my own instincts and thoughts after prayer; Scripture reading; and the advice and witness of other Christians.

In recent years, I've been impressed especially with how God has used fellow believers to help me expand my own spiritual horizons. These spiritual brothers and sisters have helped me discipline myself to follow Christ without equivocation. For a long time, I tried to be a "Lone Ranger" Christian, who attended church fairly regularly, but rarely discussed deep spiritual and personal problems with other believers. But something was missing. I needed others to share the joy of answered prayer, to advise and support me when I stepped into strange spiritual waters and doubted God's power to sustain.

Also, when I tried to operate in a spiritual vacuum, it was too easy to rationalize and play games with God. I found myself trying to fool Him with a variety of ruses: "It seems okay to pad expense accounts because God knows it's customary with this company to get a little extra income . . . there's no need for me to try to repair my relationship with this guy— God expects everybody to have a few enemies . . . after I accumulate a little nest egg, I'll be more secure and able to devote more time to God's work . . ."

As I lived my life of spiritual isolation, these rationalizations actually seemed convincing to me. But then I started to take seriously the Scriptural admonitions to get involved in fellowship with other members of the Christian community. Three other serious Christian men agreed to meet with me weekly for prayer, Bible reading, and sharing personal concerns. The change in my relationship to Christ was startling and immediate, and my spiritual growth escalated. The fantasies I had been constructing and the games I had been playing to avoid God's demands fell down like paper houses as serious Christian brothers smiled ironically, shook their heads, and revealed the hypocrisy and rationalization I knew were covering up the truth for my life. When I was honest enough to lay my problems on the table, for all to see, invariably one of my fellow believers would have an insight that added a dimension to my Christian experience—an insight I would probably never have discovered on my own.

So I've become convinced that God speaks to me through other Christians in ways that He may never speak to me alone. There is an immediate bond of spiritual kinship that ties all the members of God's family together—even "spiritual relatives" who have never met before. The comprehensive way in which the Spirit works to overcome difference in social backgrounds was revealed to me as I started interviewing celebrities who are also Christians. Movie and television stars, pop singers and super athletes had always seemed to exist in a rarefied realm, far removed from my own sphere of experience and friendships. I never imagined it might be possible to sit down with famous, internationally known figures and immediately embark on a soul-searching discussion about their deepest concerns, doubts, and joys. Outside of Christ, I think such an encounter probably *is* impossible. But when I identified myself as a fellow believer and explained to these celebrities that I'd like to sit down and share spiritual concerns with them for a book, more than a dozen responded enthusiastically.

Almost without exception, those I talked with were as open as many of the members of my own New York City prayer group. Our discussions focused first on their individual conversion and renewal experiences—the "moments of truth" when they turned from their separation from God and affirmed a new, Christ-centered existence. We then branched out into an exploration of the individual character of their walks with God.

Conversion, as William James put it, is "the process, gradual

xii

or sudden, by which a self hitherto divided, and consciously wrong, inferior and unhappy, becomes unified and consciously right, superior and happy, in consequence of its firmer hold upon religious realities" (*The Varieties of Religious Experience,* Random House, New York, 1902, 1929, p. 186). Sometimes the individuals I interviewed described their significant adult religious experience as a "renewal" of an earlier childhood conversion, but, in any case, the effect on their lives usually appeared to entail a dramatic change in their relationship with God and other people.

I was especially impressed with the many similarities, or universal points of reference, that surfaced in these Christian commitments. For example, the fact that I do some of my most effective praying under the shower in the mornings made me feel a little self-conscious, and even rather weird—until I learned that "Galloping Gourmet" Graham Kerr and Noel Paul Stookey, of the old Peter, Paul and Mary singing group, also talk to God in the tub.

Because each of these encounters with well-known believers changed my life in some way, I want to invite you to partake of the same experience. Join me now in retracing the trails trod by celebrities who have professed an intention to subordinate their ample stores of fame and fortune to Jesus Christ.

# On the Trail
# of God

# Chapter 1

# "Where Your Treasure Is . . ."

## WILLIAM DOONER

As I sipped tea in an elegant parlor of the Culloden Hotel, on the outskirts of Belfast, Northern Ireland, I still could not quite overcome my amazement at the man sitting across from me. Bill Dooner, I knew, was a self-made multimillionaire, but he didn't act or talk like any highly successful businessman I had ever known.

His short beard, wavy collar-length hair, and impish grin reminded me more of one of Robin Hood's merry men than of a twentieth-century wheeler-dealer who, at age forty-four, owned a controlling interest in seven major American corporations. As we munched our tiny tea sandwiches, he casually drew illustrative anecdotes from his experiences as a drunken Bowery bum, as a civil rights activist, and as a close friend of Christian leaders like Leighton Ford, Billy Graham's associate evangelist.

The occasion that had brought us together was Dooner's latest project as an activist Christian. He had become deeply concerned about the conflict between Protestants and Catholics in Northern Ireland, so he decided to do something about it. He devoted a great deal of time and nearly twenty thousand dollars of his own money to sponsor a "Love One Another" evangelistic tour of Northern Ireland by a team of singers and speakers from the colorful Jews for Jesus movement. His reasoning was that a nondenominational Jewish-Christian group would find it easier than any other to relate meaningfully to the intensely sectarian Northern Irish. Because I had collaborated with the movement's founder, Moishe Rosen, on the book *Jews for Jesus,* I had been invited to accompany them on the campaign.

Even though Bill Dooner and I had been together constantly for more than a week at the time that we relaxed in the Culloden, he was still something of a mystery man to me. I had picked up only bits and pieces of his background as we had taken refuge from terrorist bombs, detoured because of shootings, and watched some of the people of Belfast and Londonderry draw closer to Christ. I asked him to give me some more details about himself and his spiritual pilgrimage, and the story that unfolded was more enthralling than any Horatio Alger epic or old-time, frog-to-prince fairy tale.

"I was born in East Harlem in New York City," he began. "My mother and father were both from Ireland, and we lived in a total of about eight tenements when I was a kid. I ran numbers [for a bookie operation], sold flowers, shined shoes in taverns. I knew a lot of kids who later became leaders in the Mafia. At age nine, I was siphoning off barrels of cider to supply two hookers, two prostitutes, who ran a little cider bar in New York. They couldn't get up in the morning to siphon those barrels, so they paid me to do it—there were two kinds of cider, hard and sweet. I'd go to school completely bombed sometimes, even though I was just in the third grade."

"Do you think you were heading for a life of crime?" I asked.

"Oh, sure," Bill replied. "Most of the kids in my neighborhood did. I was arrested eight times—mostly situations related to my drinking. Once I wrecked a bar on Madison Avenue—put my hand through a jukebox. Another time I got into a brawl with some cops. I was barred from most of the bars on Third and Lexington avenues. To get money for drinks, I'd sell my blood to New York hospitals. I remember on one occasion I gave blood out of my left arm at a blood line at Bellevue Hospital, and immediately drank up the five dollars I got for it. Then the same day I hopped on the back bumper of

2

a bus and hitched a ride uptown to another hospital where I gave more blood out of my other arm."

Dooner's problem with alcoholism became a serious threat to his life one night when he got into a fight with a cab driver, and two policemen moved in to arrest him. "I started running down the street, and the cops began firing at me," he recalled. "I slipped down on the street and ripped open my pants and knee, but as it happened that was a blessing in disguise. I found out later that the cop was going to try to kill me with his next shot."

He managed to avoid an indictment by swearing on a Bible at a grand jury hearing that he would never take another drink in New York City. But he was told by the prosecutor that he would have to serve an indeterminate sentence at Rockland State Hospital if he was arrested again for drinking in the city. In fact, he said, his alcoholism was such a "serious disease" that he broke his pledge and did continue to drink for a while, but something was happening inside him. Somehow, he was beginning to realize that if he didn't change his ways, he would destroy himself. He had already spent time as a patient at Bellevue and other hospitals as a result of alcoholic convulsions. He later was admitted to the Rockefeller Institute for Medical Research as a "research patient." "The only way you get in there is that you're a specimen," he explained. "You have to be disturbed, and I *was* far gone."

The turning point of Dooner's life occurred in April 1955, when he was twenty-three years old. "My mother had left enough money on the bureau for me to pay the gas and electric bill," he recalled. "I went down to pay the bill, which was about fifteen dollars, but as I walked down the street, I passed a bar. I looked inside and saw a guy I knew drinking by himself, so I went inside. I had forty or fifty cents, and I said to myself, 'I'll have a couple of beers and then go to pay the bill.' Well, you know what happened. I got to drinking with him and drank all day long until one o'clock the next morning. But something strange happened. I didn't get drunk."

He returned home, went to bed, and the next morning he joined a fellowship of reformed alcoholics. God became a regular part of Bill Dooner's life in this fellowship, and except for one lapse in 1955, during which he ended up on Chicago's Skid

Row for six weeks, he hasn't touched a drink for more than twenty years.

"What do you think changed the direction of your life?" I asked.

"My mother's prayers," he responded quickly, and I had to admit I couldn't see any other explanation.

The sobriety which God gave Dooner freed him to develop the incredible talents for business that had been literally bottled up inside him for so long. He founded or bought several billboard companies, including Cardinal Outdoor and Boxell Signs; restaurant chains, like the Hen House; gas stations; and motel companies, such as the Royal Scotsman. His native humanitarian instincts also got him involved in civil rights activities in the Midwest during the 1960s. But something essential was still missing from his spiritual life—a personal relationship with Jesus Christ.

Dooner recognized this lack in 1974 when he and his wife, Ellie, a deeply committed Christian, traveled to Israel with evangelist Leighton Ford, Ford's wife Jean, and several mutual friends. Bill had become friendly with Ford several years before, when they had met on a vacation in Colorado. While in Israel, Dooner was particularly impressed during a trip to a prison where Jesus is said to have been held before his crucifixion. "It hit me all of a sudden; it came home to me because I'd been listening to Bible stories on this trip," Dooner said. "I never had doubts about Jesus, but I never paid much attention to the real purpose why He was here. As I opened my mind more and read life into the Bible, I began to think, 'Wow, this isn't just a piece of history. It isn't just something out of a catechism. It's a *personal* thing. Jesus came here for a purpose, and He's here today.'"

He also experienced a healing of a worrisome broken bone in his foot immediately after a Christian friend prayed over him. This renewed emphasis on Christ in his life culminated in 1975 as Bill drove toward a condominium he owned at Grandfather Mountain, Tennessee. "I was in a conflict, confused about personal and business decisions I had to make," he remembered. "Ellie kept telling me, 'If you have a problem, take it and turn it over to the Holy Spirit.' As I sat in my car with this tremendous sense of despair, I got sick and tired of being sick and

4

tired. I finally invited Christ to come into my life. I just said, 'Come into my life and take a small piece of my heart,' and the car filled up like an air bag. It was both a physical and emotional sensation. I started crying, and I can count the number of times in my life that I've cried. I almost beat my car to Grandfather Mountain, as I was grasped by this sense of serenity and peace of mind. Things really started to change in my life after that."

One dramatic change was that God began to speak to Dooner more directly through the Scriptures. He had found himself thinking more and more about the situation in Northern Ireland, and then during a lengthy private prayer session his eye came to rest on Isaiah 61:5: "Aliens shall stand and feed your flocks, foreigners shall be your plowmen and vinedressers . . ." Could God be saying something to him about foreigners in Northern Ireland? he wondered.

Dooner began to sense he could use his billboard expertise to proclaim Jesus' message of love to the feuding northern Irish. Suddenly everything seemed to come together. God appeared to be telling him to put the Christian message on billboards in Belfast, so he ordered fifteen with the words "I love you, is that okay? Jesus C." His decision was confirmed when a Christian businessman from Belfast directed him to the Living Bible version of Habakkuk 2:2: ". . . the Lord said to me, 'Write my answer on a billboard, large and clear . . .'" But Dooner needed a sponsor's imprint on the signs—an imprint which would be the least likely to aggravate the volatile Ulster religious prejudices. His thoughts wandered to a conversation in which he had heard about the importance for Biblical prophecy of the Jews' return to Israel.

"I thought, 'Wouldn't it be interesting to get some Jewish organization, which is also Christian, to put their name on the billboards,'" he said.

So he embarked on a search for his "foreigners," a Jewish-Christian group in the United States, to sponsor the signs and perhaps even to launch an evangelistic crusade. After about thirty long-distance calls to various organizations, he settled on Moishe Rosen and the Jews for Jesus. They agreed not only to the billboard imprint, but also to a one-week evangelistic tour of Northern Ireland during Easter of 1976. Dooner became

5

convinced in retrospect that God was leading him through these Bible passages and conversations with other Christians, because only a nondenominational Jewish-Christian group seemed capable of remaining above the usual Protestant-Catholic conflict that plagues most peace efforts in Ulster. "How can you ask a Jew if he's Catholic or Protestant?"—that was the question that kept coming back to him and convinced him he was on the right track.

As I sat in the Culloden Hotel that evening at the end of the campaign, I knew it would take time to evaluate completely the full impact of the effort by Dooner and the Jews for Jesus. But I was already convinced of the success of the mission as I recalled the thousands of happy faces of those who had listened on the streets of Belfast and Londonderry to the songs of hope in Christ; those who had taken off their socks and shoes to participate in public foot-washings; and those who had heard and seen the Gospel presented by the Jewish-Christian evangelists on Belfast radio and television.

None of the deepest problems of Northern Ireland had been solved, of course. Our departure from Londonderry was delayed one afternoon as two terrorist bombs shattered the afternoon quiet. The next day on the campus of Queens University in Belfast, the Jews for Jesus, assisted by sympathetic Christian friends from Northern Ireland, calmly washed the feet of various pedestrians as smoke and ashes from a nearby factory bombing filled the air. Even as Bill Dooner and I sat comfortably drinking our tea, we both knew our hotel was one of the last that had escaped terrorist attacks. A guard was on duty outside, and concertina wire surrounded the grounds.

But despite the war-zone atmosphere, I knew the love of Christ had been slipping through the battlements of Ulster during the past week. One incident in particular stuck in my mind. The Jews for Jesus singers had decided to give a street concert on the site of a bombed-out pub in the Shankill, a Protestant ghetto in Belfast. As they set up their sound equipment, a thin, freckled-faced young boy, wearing ragged, dirty clothes and ripped old shoes, wandered over and quickly made friends with the American strangers. He said his name was Samuel, and my first impression was that he was a Charles Dickens character come to life.

Bill Dooner quickly adopted him for the afternoon and learned that he had lost his hearing in one ear after being knocked to the ground when a terrorist bomb had destroyed a business down the street. A long scar on the side of his head testified to the truth of the boy's story. Dooner was particularly distressed by the condition of Samuel's shoes, so he decided to do something about it.

"I need to buy a pair of new shoes, Samuel, and I wonder if you'd show me where the nearest shoe store is?" Bill said.

"Sure," the boy replied, and they walked together to a store about a block away.

Dooner looked briefly at a couple of pairs of shoes, but then he said to the salesman, "You know, I just remembered these shoes I'm wearing now are new, and I'm breaking them in. I'm afraid it might be unfair to put these shoes of mine in a closet because they might get lonely there."

The salesman may have been disconcerted by this remark, but Samuel was listening intently and agreeing with every word.

"What size shoes do you wear, Samuel?" Dooner then asked the boy.

"Size three," he replied quickly.

"Well, how about it? Do you see anything *you* might like?" Dooner asked with a twinkle in his eye. They left the store with a shiny new pair of size-three shoes, and contented smiles on both their faces.

That incident told me a great deal about Bill Dooner's approach to the Christian faith and the way he believes in applying his ample funds to further the cause of Christ. He is, above all, an activist. He would never be satisfied playing the role of an armchair benefactor who dispenses funds from afar to the needy. By getting involved with Samuel as a friend *before* buying him those shoes, he helped preserve the boy's sense of dignity and worth as an individual. And by throwing himself into witnessing and tract-passing with the Jews for Jesus—in addition to footing their bills—he encouraged them and helped their cause much more than he would have by just donating some dollars.

As I watched Bill Dooner during that Easter week, I couldn't help but remember the Apostle Paul's statement in Romans 12:8 that the ability to contribute liberally of one's worldly

7

possessions is a gift from God. In another context, Paul warned Timothy that "the love of money is the root of all evils," but he went on to say that rich Christians have a definite place in God's scheme of things: "They are to do good, to be rich in good deeds, liberal and generous . . ." (1 Timothy 6:10, 18).

Bill Dooner seemed to be fulfilling these passages of Scripture in his work in Northern Ireland, and I knew I was learning a great deal from him myself. God has given each of us certain gifts, and He means for us to be responsible managers of the money, talent, or time that is ours. As long as we put God first and allow Him to direct us in the use of our gifts, life will fall into a peaceful, purposeful pattern. Or as Jesus said in Matthew 6:19–21, "Do not lay up for yourselves treasures on earth, where moth and rust consume and where thieves break in and steal, but lay up for yourselves treasures in heaven, where neither moth nor rust consumes and where thieves do not break in and steal. For where your treasure is, there will your heart be also."

William Dooner seemed to me to have his treasure in the right place.

Chapter 2

# "If the Salt Has Lost Its Savour . . ."

## GRAHAM AND TREENA KERR

Graham and Treena Kerr—the old "Galloping Gourmet" television cooking team—made one overwhelming, indelible first impression on me: they are radical followers of Christ. Although some may find their spiritual extremism to be frustrating, more often it hit me like a breath of fresh air in the often uninspiring corridors of stale church tradition and spiritual compromise.

The Kerrs' unequivocal devotion to Christ struck me the very first time I spoke to Graham on the telephone. Instead of saying, "Hello," he and everyone else in his household says, "Praise Jesus!" It's somewhat disconcerting at first. I don't remember my initial reaction—maybe a stutter or a nervous laugh. After I got to know them better, I asked Graham why they answer this way.

"Jesus is the most important person in this house," he replied in his familiar British accent. "We occupy this house because He has permitted us to do so. Therefore it's only proper that we should answer the phone in His name. Instead of saying, 'Hi!' we just say, 'Praise Jesus!'

"Of course, we don't know what the response will be. When you pick the phone up, there's that little decision you have to

9

make every time because you don't know who is on the other end. And when you say, 'Praise Jesus,' there's that little hesitation on the other end. Some of us say, 'Praise the Lord,' and some say, 'Praise Jesus.' But I do think there is a subtle difference. When we say the word Jesus, that is the name above all other names. It leaves no doubt in anybody's mind about what is happening. That name is so powerful that it always elicits a negative response from those people who are not with Him. If you go out and ask for money in the name of compassion for those who are dying in the Third World, or in the name of public righteousness, you can always pick up a whole dollar from someone. But if you introduce the name of Jesus, you get only twenty-five cents on the dollar. So in a way, on first contact with people on the phone, we like to sort the wheat from the chaff before we even know who is there."

At first, I wasn't quite sure whether they regarded me as wheat or chaff, and that made me somewhat uncomfortable. It's not that they were ungracious or unfriendly; on the contrary, they didn't hesitate to invite me down to their rambling colonial mansion in Easton, Maryland. And Graham, though he was suffering from a bad cold, welcomed me with open arms when I landed at the small local airport in a four-seater commuter plane.

My main problem was a sense of defensiveness—probably completely unjustified—that developed as we sat down to have lunch at their home. Graham gave a prayer as we all held hands at the table, and then he pulled out a huge Bible. He began to read from Matthew 7:21, where Jesus says, "Not every one who says to me, 'Lord, Lord,' shall enter the kingdom of heaven, but he who does the will of my Father who is in heaven."

"I guess that means that some people even today may claim to know the Lord, but really don't have a saving knowledge of Him," Graham observed tentatively.

"I think that's definitely true," I said as we dug into our salads. "I'm sure our churches must be full of people who give lip service to the lordship of Christ, but don't actually believe in Him and follow Him as their Savior."

Then it suddenly struck me that perhaps Graham had read that passage to feel me out—maybe even to help convert me if

10

I were one of those people who give lip service to Jesus, yet have not really made an unequivocal commitment. Probably there was no reason for me to think this way, but, in any case, I felt self-conscious. And I found myself reading judgmental meanings into what they were saying to me during the rest of the lunch.

Of course, I'm not saying the Kerrs harbored any such attitudes at all. As I indicated, my main problem was likely in my own head. But I sensed in them a slight uncertainty, which I suppose is normal when a stranger asks to be accepted as your spiritual brother. I continued to feel a little apprehensive when we settled down after lunch on their sunny front porch. But whatever their private opinions of my spiritual condition, they didn't hesitate to open up to me at once—especially Graham. Treena is a little more distant, more reserved, and it takes her a while to warm up. But soon they were both describing their life histories to me in minute detail and garnishing many points with tantalizing culinary images.

They were extremely successful during the 1960s and early 1970s on the "Galloping Gourmet" television series, with Treena as producer and Graham as the grinning, outrageous, world-renowned cook. Graham, a tall, vigorous man in his early forties, became famous for his enormous physical energy —bounding over chairs with a bottle of wine in hand—and for what he now calls his "lavatory schoolboy humor."

Recalling his pre-Christian career life, Graham said, "I was always a little inebriated, and people used to watch to see if I would fall drunk into my soufflé. I drank throughout the whole program. People used to laugh at me, and I liked being laughed at. I was a tippler then, but now I don't drink or even use wine for cooking. I will not use alcohol in any way, shape or form. The reason is that I believe I might encourage someone else to stumble. Someone might say, 'Look, he's a Christian and he drinks.' There's no way I can do that, and I don't miss it at all. I'm much happier now without alcohol, but I didn't know that at the time."

Graham's antics enabled them to put about $2 million in the bank, buy a beautiful home and a half-million-dollar yacht, and live like royalty. But the material wealth didn't bring inner peace and satisfaction or marital bliss. As our discussion continued, it became clear that, in a spiritual sense reminiscent of Jesus' words in Matthew 5:13, the "salt [had] lost his savour" in the Kerrs' cooking career and home life.

"We never had any fun with that money," Treena recalls. "The more popular the series got and the more famous Graham got, the more I resented it. I knew it was better for Graham to be in the foreground, but I felt great competition and jealousy. I got harder and harder. You see, I loved acting when I was younger, and I was a good drama and comedy actress. The theater used to make me feel wanted. But when an actress is in it for ego's sake and nothing else, she can never find real satisfaction."

I told her that because both my wife and I are in journalism, I understood how tough it could be for a husband and wife who are in similar fields to work together. "There's always some tension when we're editing each other's work, or collaborating on something," I said.

Treena nodded knowingly and continued: "It got so bad that everywhere I went, I saw this silly face of his—in bookstores, in rehearsals, and on the television screen. I became very resentful because I was working as hard as he was but getting no kudos as the producer. I was nominated two years in a row for an Emmy, but nobody cared, nobody was a bit interested. We'd be interviewed, and people would ask, 'What do *you* do, Mrs. Kerr, while your husband is working?' "

Treena cringed as she recalled her reactions in those days. Her inner anguish had also been aggravated by serious physical problems. Both Treena and Graham were severely injured in an auto accident in California in 1971. Then Treena had to undergo a serious lung operation. Somehow, material success didn't seem to be providing the happiness they had expected, so they decided to try to escape from the pressures of civilization.

"We went on a dreadful boat trip, back and forth across the Atlantic Ocean for two years," she said, shaking her head. At the height of their fame and fortune, Treena and Graham fitted out their half-million-dollar yacht and, with two hired crewmen and the three Kerr children, set out for an extended "vacation."

"It was absolute murder," Graham interjected. "There weren't really any fights, but I can only remember two days of fun, and Treena can't remember that much."

12

"Graham was perpetually demanding that we get to a certain place at a certain time," Treena said. "We were dressed as a crew in special professional uniforms with symbols and name tags. Graham had things so organized that he just had to lift a hand or a finger—no voice commands at all—and his will would be done. I didn't like it at all."

Graham smiled sheepishly at this comment: "I got some tremendous charges out of that boat," he remarked. "But real fun has a follow-through, and that experience was never fun to look back on. The pleasure just came in short spurts. We never got together as a family. We tried and failed."

I had heard that Graham had gotten involved in affairs with other women during this period, and even though it was an uncomfortable subject, I knew I had to ask them about it. "There has been some mention of the fact that you were involved with a woman before your conversion—what about that?" I asked.

"There were quite a few women, but I only knew about two of them," Treena said frankly. "I had a breakdown and had to go into the hospital because of the suffering from the hurts and the disastrous feelings of the first one."

"I was extremely agitated too at that time because Treena had to be put into a hospital," Graham said. "I never once enjoyed the process of being unfaithful. The first time it caught me by surprise. The second time, I did it deliberately because I felt I wasn't loved. I believe most unfaithfulness is retaliation. I hated myself and did the same thing again."

I was amazed at their openness and honesty about such intimate details of their married life. If anything like this had happened to me, I don't know that I could have talked about it so freely for general public consumption. But celebrities, who are always in the public eye, seem more inclined to talk about the private things in their lives, especially if they are Christians talking to a fellow Christian. In my small prayer group, I know I feel comfortable sharing intimate things with my brothers in Christ because I realize my experiences and prayers may well help them in their own spiritual growth. On a much broader scale, famous Christians seem to sense that if they disclose personal things that show how God has acted in their lives, many of their fans may be encouraged and assisted in their walk with Christ.

The pressures on Treena built up so much that she recalled, "Sometimes I wished I'd die. If I died, it would be out of the way. I didn't love Graham, didn't trust him, had lost all respect for him. When you lose respect for your husband and still work with him, you become dominating. You work to gain power over him, and you get his respect but not his love. Actually, I had lost respect for all males. I thought they were all a lot of sex-ridden beasts."

This dissatisfaction was churning inside Treena when they returned from the cruise and bought their colonial mansion in Easton, Maryland. Her frustration eventually caused Treena to get hooked on drugs. "Somebody left me some speed, and I was on strong pain-killers because of the lingering effects of the auto accident and lung operation. I'd take marijuana, about twelve valiums a day, speed—all without Graham's knowledge. I had no pain, but I also had no meaning in my life. The speed gave me a high and made me feel good. The valium was supposed to keep me from losing my temper. But my temper was uncontrollable. I had a tremendous desire to pick up knives and stab people, to run through glass windows. And I was racked by these violent visions. The more pills I took, the less it helped. I was terrified of anything mechanical or male. If I heard of somebody being raped, I'd weep for days."

Treena also thought seriously about committing suicide, but "the only thing that kept me from that was a twenty-year belief in reincarnation. I was afraid I'd come back to earth in worse form, or have to go through the same things again. I couldn't bear the thought of that. Three times I thought seriously about killing myself, and once I actually took eight or ten sleeping pills. My kids were all scared of me. I didn't like me and they didn't like me."

Unbeknownst to Treena, in the midst of all her misery her black maid, Ruth Turner, had been fasting and praying for her salvation. One day, when Treena was complaining about her lot in life, Ruth said, "Why don't you give your problems to God?"

Thoroughly disillusioned by the failure of other remedies and not completely sure what she was doing, Treena finally said, "Okay, God, you take it. I can't do it." For the next few days, her problems seemed to get better. "I let Graham do the talk-

14

ing," she remembers. "I didn't say anything. For some reason, everything seemed to be improving.

"Then Ruthie said, 'Why don't you get baptized in water?' I laughed and said, 'I don't believe in that sort of thing.' She said, 'Have you ever been baptized?' I said, 'I was christened as a child.' But she replied, 'No, I mean complete submersion in water. That's dying to your sins.'"

Treena decided she had better set some things straight with Ruth: "I told her, 'I don't believe in Jesus.' Then a little voice in my head reminded me what I used to like to do most when I lost my temper: I used to want to go swimming or have a shower or something—anything to do with water. So why not baptism? My doctor was already advising Graham I should be committed for my own and the children's safety—so why not give Jesus and His baptism a chance?"

The TV producer finally agreed to be baptized, and a few days later she and her daughter Tessa followed an excited Ruth into an all-black church in Bethlehem, Maryland. "They were banging on tambourines and drums, and I was really excited, though I didn't know why," Treena said. "Tessa wanted to go home—she was horrified. But I said, 'No, I want to see this through.' The pastor asked me if I knew what I was doing, and I said, 'Of course I know!' even though I didn't know anything. He said, 'You might not get it,' and I said, 'Of course I'm going to get it!'—but I had no idea what I was going to get."

The pastor had the congregation stand up, and the people started to pray for her. "I got this feeling in the pit of my tummy—bump! bump! bump! Suddenly it came right up into my throat and I couldn't breathe. I thought I was suffocating. It was as though somebody had put a hand over my mouth. Then this loud noise hit me, and I fell on the ground. Water was literally pouring out of my eyes—not ordinary tears, but literally streams, like two taps of water. I thought, 'What on earth is going on!' It was water, water, water pouring out. And I said, 'I'm sorry, Jesus, forgive me, Jesus!'

"Nobody took notice of me except Tessa, who had turned very green. She said later she went to pick me up and take me out of the church because she was horrified that I should fall down in front of all these people—'What would Daddy say?' she wondered. But she was knocked off her feet, onto a nearby

15

pew by the force that was surrounding me. It really frightened her, but I felt quite empty and peaceful. I couldn't wait to get into the water and be baptized."

After the congregation had finished their prayer, Treena put on a white gown and stepped into the extremely cold water in the church's baptistry. "I thought, as I was going down, that I was going to come out new. I was so light when I came up. I don't even remember walking up onto the steps, but I do remember thinking about Jesus. Then the pastor asked me, 'Have you received it?' I said, 'I don't think so.' He said, 'You'll know when you receive it. Would you like to tarry?' I asked, 'What is that?' He said, 'Tarry means wait for the baptism of the Holy Spirit.' I said, 'I might as well as long as I'm here, mightn't I?'"

So Treena knelt in front of the preacher and murmured, "Thank you, Jesus," over and over. She was on her knees for so long that they still hurt her four days later. "I thought, 'This is really ridiculous,'" she said. "The sweat was running down my face. The people were singing songs, banging tambourines. I began to think I was really off my head. Then this bright light came into my face, and I thought, 'Now they've turned up the church lights to make me think I'm getting what I'm supposed to be getting.' When I opened my eyes, though, I saw this man, all in white. The smile on that face was the smile of all the love you could possibly see. I mean, just complete love of everything. The man put out his hand and touched my heart, and then he disappeared."

She was still filled with wonder when the pastor interrupted by asking, "Have you received it yet?"

"I don't know," Treena replied, "but I've just seen somebody."

But the preacher said, "Well, never mind, you come back another day."

When Treena stood up, she said she felt "stupefied, didn't know what was going on." She noticed Tessa had left, so she went outside and found the girl at the car. Tessa cried, "Oh, Mommy, that's so awful. It's evil there—evil, evil, evil!"

"Well, I feel pretty neat," Treena said mysteriously. She found she was so full of energy that she drove all the way home without a touch of exhaustion.

In retrospect, Treena says, "I know now that it was Jesus I saw in that church, but I didn't know it then. I did know something special had happened, though I didn't have any experience speaking in tongues at the time. The next morning, when I saw my face in the mirror, it looked better than it had for months. And a voice seemed to say to me, 'You have it.' 'It' was clearly the baptism of the Spirit, and I knew then that I had it. Two months later, I received the gift of tongues, even though I'd never heard anyone speak in tongues before. My mouth kept going into funny shapes and I wondered what was happening. I tried to speak, but gibberish came out, and then suddenly I started to sing in a completely new, unknown language. Now, I can talk to God in this language whenever I like."

Visions similar to Treena's, accompanied by bright, often colorful flashes of light, have been fairly common in dramatic Christian conversion and renewal experiences. The Apostle Paul, of course, was temporarily blinded by a bright light in his encounter with Christ on the road to Damascus (Acts 9). Charles Finney, the great nineteenth-century American evangelist and president of Oberlin College, wrote of his conversion, ". . . the glory of God shone upon and round about me in a manner almost marvelous . . . A light perfectly ineffable shone in my soul, that almost prostrated me on the ground . . . This light seemed like the brightness of the sun in every direction. It was too intense for the eyes . . ." (For a fuller account of Finney's experience, and similar incidents, see William James, *The Varieties of Religious Experience,* Random House, New York, 1902, 1929, pp. 246ff.)

A radical change in Treena's inner self soon was manifested in her improved relationships with the rest of the family. Graham didn't quite know what to make of it, and Treena avoided telling him anything about her experience. Before her conversion, Graham said, "There used to be a row in our home every day. It was really hellish. She would be frothing at the mouth, and staring at me with wide, startled, bulging eyes. On some occasions, if she had had a knife, she would have driven it right into me. I weigh nearly twice as much as Treena, but there was no way I wasn't terrified of her when she went into one of her rages."

But suddenly there were no more rages. There were no more arguments. A reservoir of love seemed to be filling up inside her. "God told me to just keep quiet," she said. "He literally told me not to say anything to Graham at all. He just told me Graham would be saved."

Graham heard about Treena's church experience at a supermarket, and he ran home to share the joke with her. But he soon learned it was no joke. She told him that she had accepted Jesus, and He had changed her life. At first Graham didn't know what to make of the situation. Finally, impressed by the change in her, he asked, "Do you want me to do what you've done?"

"No, I don't think you need it," Treena replied, and that made Graham feel relieved that he didn't have to "toe the line" to please her. But three months later, he left on a television production trip to Canada, and Treena gave him a Bible, which he read because he knew she was reading one. He missed her and wanted somehow to feel he was closer to her. He also began to pray rote prayers—"God bless Daddy, God bless Mummy . . ."—but nothing happened.

Finally, one night in a Canadian hotel room, "I lost my temper," he said. "I fell to my knees and said, 'I'm fed up to the back teeth with this stupid nonsense about religion! I'm reading this Bible, praying every night, and it's doing absolutely nothing! I feel worse now than I did before. I'm fed up, and I want to go to sleep! I want You—if You're anywhere at all—to do something about this! *Right now!*'"

At that point he shook his Bible at the ceiling, and "without realizing it, I got both my hands in the air. It was the first time I'd done anything sensible. We think the hands are important—get the thinking agent, the brain, down below them and it's easier to communicate with God. I closed my eyes and was really feeling hostile. In a demanding tone, I asked God again, 'What do I have to say? Tell me what I have to say!' Then I opened my eyes, and I saw the part of the ceiling in the corner, where everything seems to meet in a cross. I just looked at that and said, 'Jesus, I love you!'—out loud.

"Up to that time, I was only addressing God [the Father]. I was striving to reach God, and I had no idea that He has a telephone exchange—Jesus Christ. I thought Jesus was just a

18

major prophet. But God gave me the answer when I asked Him. He put into my mouth what I had to say to be saved. He gave me the word, 'Jesus.' I never had any previous thoughts about going to Jesus. It was just a matter of asking, and the word was there in my mouth."

A great wave of emotion followed, and Graham began to talk conversationally to God through his tears. "The physical experience for me was like screwing in one of those sparklet bulbs—a little carbonated air container that you use to make soda water," he explained. "It discharges millions of little bubbles and aerates the water. That's the way I felt—as though a spiritual sparklet had been screwed into my ear, and every part of my body was enlivened. I felt totally effervescent.

"The spiritual experience, on the other hand, was a wave of gratitude for the experience of salvation which Jesus had accomplished for me on the cross. I also had a sense of relief in knowing that I had been delivered from my awful past and that my forty years of ignorance had ended."

He didn't speak in tongues at this point, but did two weeks later on Easter Sunday morning in 1975. The conversions of their three children, Andrew, Tessa, and Kareena, followed soon after, and the Kerrs found they had embarked on the greatest adventure of their adventure-packed lives.

After their conversions, they said, they immediately became deeply involved in what Graham calls "supernatural" expressions of their faith. For example, he was still ailing from the California auto accident injuries, and he had a $3 million lawsuit pending against a trucking company. "My neck was out about a half inch, and my left side was partially paralyzed," he said. But then he was "slain in the Spirit" during a "miracle meeting" conducted by Charles and Frances Hunter in Toronto. In other words, he fell to the floor and was "literally held there by the power of God." He says his physical problems were "healed instantly."

"At the same meeting, I was asked to hold on to a man's hand at the end of a row of about thirty people," he recalled. "They were all saying, 'Praise the Lord!' and 'Hallelujah!' and I just said in a conversational way, 'Let the Holy Spirit come upon these people.' The whole row fell over simultaneously.

"Well, I was tickled pink about that. I said, 'Hey, neat!' So I

19

looked for another complete row, and said again, 'Holy Spirit, come upon these people!' But nothing happened. I decided I wasn't pious enough, so I said it again. Nothing."

"You were trying to do it under your own power?" I asked.

"Yes. I was trying to do it myself, when actually it was the Holy Spirit doing it through me," he explained. "I was only about ten days old in the Lord at that time."

One of the most difficult things Graham had to do after his conversion was to learn to be completely open and honest with Treena—even about his past extramarital escapades. (Claiming that "God is quite precise," he prefers to call them "adulteries.") He told the story as the three of us were still soaking in the sunshine on the porch of his Maryland home. "I knew we couldn't minister to others in marriage unless I confessed this to Treena, and I didn't know how I was going to do it. It happened to me one night when I was showing my son, Andrew, something about submitting to God. The others had credited me with becoming the priest of the family, and I was delighted to show my spiritual authority. Treena had always ruled the roost before, because I had blown it."

Treena nodded. "Yes, you *had* blown it!"

"But as I prayed that night with the family for deliverance from the demon of spiritual superiority, I began to wonder how I could expect to help Andrew and the others when I myself had such a series of unconfessed sins," Graham continued. "I started to tell them how I had developed a spirit of retaliation against Treena, and it became clear I was getting closer and closer to the complete confession. So I stopped, and Treena said, 'There's something else, isn't there?' I said, 'Yes, there is, but it's something I can't say in the flesh, and you can't receive in the flesh. It's something I can only say and you can only receive in the Spirit.'" Then Graham, pausing in his narrative, turned to Treena and smiled. "You didn't have a glimmer, did you?" They looked at each other so intimately, it almost seemed that either they had forgotten I was there, or they had begun to accept me as a member of the family.

She shook her head and laughed. "No, I thought maybe you'd had another child or were a homosexual or something. All these things went through my mind. But it was funny—even with those awful thoughts, it didn't matter to me."

Then Graham returned to his story: "I began to confess the whole thing. I actually started to sob, and the kids—Tessa, Andrew, and Kareena—politely withdrew. I broke completely —couldn't even look at Treena. I knew in my flesh she couldn't take what I was about to say. My confession to her was going to blow everything apart—Jesus . . . the whole thing—I just knew it. I didn't have enough faith in Treena's spirit to understand how strong she was.

"But as I cried out my confession, full of self-pity and agony as well as relief, I opened my eyes and sought hers. Her eyes were like those great space probes they have at NASA, great parabolic things, huge deep saucers. She was crying, tears welling up in her eyes, making them even larger than life. And I believe that when Jesus looked on people with forgiveness, it had to be the way Treena looked that evening. I saw Jesus in my wife's eyes."

We all fell silent for a moment or two, and I could tell they were still savoring that profound encounter. Then Treena sighed and said, "I felt terribly relieved and sorry he should have had to keep it back so long. It didn't bother me one little bit. I said, 'Jesus, it doesn't matter what it is—it's in the past.' Even the thought that he might have had another child didn't bother me."

"I really understood what forgiveness was," Graham said. "I was afraid, but the perfect love of Jesus drove the fear away. That was the exciting thing."

As they discussed their marriage, I recalled that Graham and Treena were planning on starting a Christian retreat center for couples with ailing marriages in Eagle, Colorado. (Graham calls it an "advance" center. "Since Jesus won," he says, "why should Christians have to retreat from the world?") "It's great you'll be able to discuss these experiences with other Christian couples," I said. "They certainly won't be able to tell you that you don't know what you're talking about."

Graham chuckled: "Well, they *can* say I'm inexperienced in certain areas. For one thing, I never beat Treena. I don't understand that problem, so we'll have to find some people who do. You know, there are Christian men who beat their wives."

"We know very little, but the Holy Spirit will help us," Treena said. "The Holy Spirit has been working incredibly with

Graham. It's really neat." She turned to him and said, "You are really becoming the priest of the family now. Really! I just think it's fantastic. When I feel myself flopping around, I know there's a complete strength there in you. Not when you get loud —but that quietness, that quiet strength of the Lord. And I tell you, I feel very, very secure. It's probably the first time in my life I've felt secure. I see now how God's used you. I had to ask God to help me love and respect you, and He did. The respect came pretty fast and the love came slower. But they're real, *really* real now. I've been meaning to say that to you."

"That's perhaps the most wonderful compliment that a Christian husband can have," Graham replied, obviously deeply moved. In a way, I felt almost like an intruder at this tender moment, but I also sensed they were happy to have me share it with them.

"I know where your ultimate trust is—in God—and it gives me security," Treena said.

"That's an example of why the power of two is so incredible —couple power," Graham mused.

"God told Graham right at the beginning that when two give their testimony together, the power is multiplied," Treena noted.

I had seen them on television together in New York, during a Christian telethon sponsored by the Lambs Club Church in Manhattan, and I agreed that their joint testimony was quite effective.

"Yet people don't realize that," Graham said. "Every pastor wants me, but they're learning they have to take Treena as part of the act. You know, sort of like Sabu and the Elephant."

"God has taught me humility," Treena said, her head slightly bowed and her hands clasped in her lap. She still seemed to be struggling with the old marital competition problem.

"Does it bother you—that many Christian leaders are mainly interested in having Graham appear at their rallies?" I asked.

"Not now," she said.

"That's gone," Graham agreed.

"But it did bother me at the beginning," Treena admitted. "I used to want to go away and cry with humiliation. I said, 'They're going to think I'm just using Graham,' but God said, 'What *are* you doing? You *are* using Him! We're *both* using

22

him! You'd never get on there without him! Now you go out there and talk into his tie.' I said, 'God, it's so humiliating.' I've only been able to do it because of Jesus. But now it doesn't hurt me any more. I know Jesus is more important. He taught me humility. You can often feel that the whole audience really wants to listen to the Galloping Gourmet, so I have to just sit there. But I start to pray in the Spirit, in tongues, and then I get a nice calmness. And I don't care what they think."

By now, I sensed that they were accepting me more confidently as a full-fledged Christian brother. There was nothing specific they'd said that made me feel this way. It was just an attitude, an openness, a feeling that they were ready to reach out to me, and include me in their own spiritual struggles. One of the struggles surfaced as the telephone rang during our conversation on their sunny front porch. It was a call from New York . . . about a crisis in their "Take Kerr" television cooking series—a crisis which was to result in their decision to end their television careers.

The roots of this problem went back into their first days as new Christians trying to find God's will. Graham had always given Cornell University a credit on his program for the help they gave him as his consultants on nutrition. But when Graham became more explicit about Jesus in his books and programs, the Cornell representatives decided they would rather not have their name associated with him. As a result, they asked to be removed from the credit lines which were televised at the end of each program. This left Graham with a hole in his credits which he somehow felt should be filled.

"I asked God about this as I was taking a shower one morning," he said. "I have this habit—and I don't want to recommend that everybody try it—but I pray under the shower every morning. I spend a lot of time in the shower, and I find it's a good time to talk with God."

"You do?" I said, surprised. "Well, *I* do too."

"You do?" Graham said happily.

"Isn't that incredible!" I replied. Finding another Christian brother to share spiritual experiences with is one thing, but one who prays in the shower to boot, well, that was almost too much.

"That's great," Graham said. "It's super—a super place. The

23

shower wakes you up so well, so that when you come out you're ready to go."

"You know, I've often wished I had a waterproofed Bible to take into the shower with me," I said.

"You can do that, in a way," he said. "You can buy Scriptures on tape, and listen to them. An interesting thing happened to me in connection with this shower thing. Someone asked me, 'Do you pray a lot?' I said, 'Oh, yes, of course'—with a considerable amount of pride, I might add. The man said, 'Good. And how much do you listen?' I said, 'I beg your pardon?' He repeated, 'How much do you listen?'

"I said, 'I don't understand.'

"So he said, once again, 'When do you listen for God's answer?' I said, 'It comes to you, doesn't it?' He said, 'Why do you think there's a delay? Why don't you listen for an answer straightaway?'

"I thought that was a pretty neat idea, so now I pray for guidance under the shower and listen while I shave. As I'm shaving, something comes into my mind, and I think about it. Sometimes I have a message such as this one: 'My words are like the beat of the dove's wings. Get to them before the hunter.' I interpret that to mean God's words are the first words that come to me. Satan pounces on them very quickly. When we pray in the Spirit, we send out important messages, and God speaks to us almost instantly. But our brain starts to move in, and Satan uses it. After I get out of that shower, I try to train myself to be obedient to the first words."

"Do you have some way of testing even those first words, to be certain they're from God?" I asked.

"Yes, I always test the first words against Scripture," Graham said. "I test everything. Now, let me tie all this into the credit problem on our televison program. God told me, as I was shaving, that He wanted a credit on my program. I remember laughing, but the idea came back to me, and I couldn't think of anything else. Then I said, 'Why not? I gave Cornell the credit, so why not God?' "

First of all, Graham wrote out a lengthy credit: "Graham Kerr wishes to acknowledge with gratitude the direction and guidance given to him in the preparation of this program by God." As Graham recalls, "It looked terrible! Just dreadful!"

Then at Treena's suggestion they decided to give God the credit by "putting His Word on the air—just a reference to a Scripture verse that related to something I'd done during the program," Graham said. As a result, a printed Bible citation— such as "Matthew 6:25"—was inserted at the end of each "Take Kerr" program, along with the other acknowledgments of those who had worked on the show. At first, Graham's distributor objected. But finally they agreed to "put the Bible passages on to see how it goes," Graham recalled.

But Graham had become unhappy with his career in general about this time. He seemed to be working more and enjoying it less. "God doesn't make you suffer, yet I was suffering with my career at this point," Graham explained. "Treena hated it because she could see how sick I was."

"Jesus' burden is easy and light, and I knew it shouldn't have been like that," Treena said. "There was no joy. God gives you the joy, but there was no joy. Graham was covered with nervous sores, and he looked terribly gray. I knew God didn't want him involved in TV at all. But everybody was saying, 'It's so important that Graham keep on TV,' so I said, 'Okay, I'm not going to mention how much I hate seeing you sick. It's in God's hands. God has to turn this off—I can't. If God wants to stop it, He'll have to do it!'"

At about this time, Graham and Treena visited the Melodyland Christian Center in Southern California for a service that was being conducted by Dr. Ralph Wilkerson. Graham told Wilkerson that he and Treena didn't want to go onto the stage, but "he felt led to pull us out," Graham said. "So there we were, standing on the platform in front of four thousand people. Ralph said, 'Well, children, how are things in your lovely household?' And I said, 'They're not good. We're working hard, and it affects us adversely. I get very tired. I work long hours. The fruit of the Spirit is not in our house because of that. I just don't know what to do.' Then Treena spoke too and she wept."

At that point, Treena asked the congregation to pray for them. Wilkerson then laid hands on both of them, and they fell down, "slain in the Spirit," on the platform. "I knew I'd been knocked off my feet by the Spirit because it had happened to me before," Graham said, reminding me of the time his neck was healed. "But there we were, flat on our backs in the middle

25

of Melodyland Church. Even though we were still confused about why we were working, I believed then God was going to fix our whole career problem."

"Being slain in the Spirit is a unique experience," Treena said. "You know you're on the floor, but you cannot move. You try to get up, but you can't. It's as though someone has a hand on your arms. You're very aware of what's going on, but you couldn't care less. You're kind of detached from yourself."

Although I'd never experienced the phenomenon they described, I was reminded somewhat of an intense encounter with God I had late one night. "It was after some guests, who had participated in a deep spiritual discussion with us, had left our apartment," I told Graham and Treena. "I sensed God was communicating to me, telling me to witness more actively for Him. The experience continued even after I went to bed. As I was lying there, it was almost as though I were floating, even though I knew I was still on the bed."

"Yes, you're aware of everything, minutely aware, yet detached," Treena said. "I wasn't afraid at all—it was a nice feeling, a feeling of being completely released."

"Treena had asked for everyone to pray for us, and I think that's the main thing that knocked us down—the power of prayer," Graham noted. "When you're in the midst of four thousand people and they're all praying for you, zeroing in on you, it's a mighty experience. You can get knocked right off your feet by all that spiritual energy.

"As I lay there on that stage, I *knew* God had fixed my career. I felt buoyant. I gave my work to God on that platform that day. I said, 'God, it's on your altar. I'm not going to reach back and take it from you, even though you know I'm a real Indian giver.' "

The very next day, Graham heard from his agents in New York. "They said the J. Walter Thompson Company, which was distributing the program, had received some complaints from local TV stations about the Scripture credits on my programs," Graham said. "The agents said, 'You'll have to take them off.' "

A bizarre "battle of the Bible" then ensued between J. Walter Thompson, the largest advertising agency in the world, and the Kerrs. Here is Graham's version of the highlights:

He told them, "We plain can't remove the verses because God told us not to." The advertising agency agreed, and Graham says he "rejoiced" because he saw God being challenged and then winning.

The Kerrs spent three months preparing a new set of programs. But as they started to record them, the J. Walter Thompson people changed their minds and ordered the verses to be taken off. When the Kerrs refused again, the agency proposed a compromise: "They said we should print the Bible passages out completely without the citation," Graham said. "But I told them the viewers might think the words came from William Shakespeare, or Jerome K. Jerome, or me. 'We must give God, the Author, the credit,' I said. Then they said we should just put in the words 'Holy Bible.' They wanted to get away from the actual Scriptural reference."

Graham objected to both these proposals, and J. Walter Thompson once again agreed to the Kerrs' original terms, to include the specific verse citations. But after the cooking series went on the air, Treena and Graham noticed that the Scripture references had been edited out.

Confronting the advertising agency again, Graham said, "We'll give you a chance to repent, gentlemen, because we feel Jesus would do the same. You put God's Word back again, and we'll continue to do business with you."

But the company came back with another compromise: "They said, 'All right, we'll replace the citations [on several hundred of the programs], but we want you never to put those verses on again,'" Graham said. "We said, 'No, we can't agree to that,' and so we eventually parted company."

As I listened to Graham's description of this controversy, I couldn't understand why the advertising company would be willing to print out the entire Bible passage, or include the phrase "Holy Bible," but would refuse so adamantly to include a simple, short, precise Scripture reference. "Isn't that strange?" I said to Graham.

"It's not strange—it's perfectly reasonable!" he retorted. "Satan will allow us to spout Scriptures. But without specific references, we, as a meditating, learning, revelation-seeking body of believers, are without any help, without the full power of the word of God. The Bible is a big book. I tell you, the specific references are absolutely vital. But imagine: here's this huge organization, this giant industry of television, finding it impossible to be able to tolerate 'Luke 12:36' or 'Matthew 6:25'! They're a battleship against a rowboat! But as I like to say, 'See Who is rowing my rowboat!'"

So the Bible battle came to a close, with Graham and Treena ending their "Take Kerr" series and their television careers as well—at least for the foreseeable future. I tried unsuccessfully to get the J. Walter Thompson Company's view on the matter. A spokesperson in their public relations department, after checking with her superiors, would only reply, "J. Walter Thompson is continuing to syndicate the program." She refused to give any substantive answers about the details of the dispute with the Kerrs.

The final footnote to the episode was written when the couple learned that some people who had relied on the production of the programs were facing financial difficulties. "I know Jesus doesn't have people suffer," Graham said. "So we went to prayer about it, and the most exciting thing happened to us. We prayed, 'Lord, what do we do? Please, what do we do?' Treena prayed in the Spirit [in tongues], and I interpreted. God said, 'Forgive them everything they owe you, and give them every program you have ever made, all the rights, all the property, all the designs, all the cookware, everything.'

"We called the people involved back and said, 'You've got the lot. We can't compromise, but we will do this because God just told us to do so. The income from the program should be sufficient to offset your losses.'"

As he spoke, I couldn't help recalling that radical, impossible idea Jesus advocated in the Sermon on the Mount (Matthew 5:40–41): ". . . if any one would sue you and take your coat, let him have your cloak as well; and if any one forces you to go one mile, go with him two miles."

But perhaps it isn't such an impossible idea after all.

As the Kerrs move forward with their marital "advance" program, they are still exploring the many dimensions of their Christian faith as a close-knit team, especially as they pray together in the evening in their prayer language, or glossolalia.

Treena's tongue has a Latin, Romantic-language sound, while Graham's "is strange, like a Russian Count," Treena says.

"There is so much the Spirit has to say," Graham declares. "The Spirit gives us a far greater vocabulary than we have in English."

"At night, we lie in bed or kneel when we pray," Treena says. "Graham goes first. Then I say my prayers out loud and finally we pray together in the Spirit, out loud."

"Have you ever felt self-conscious about praying together?" I asked. "Some couples do."

"That's sad, too, because praying together is the most unique ministry God has for us," Graham replied. "We don't feel self-conscious at all, and it's so beautiful."

"You can talk to God about each other's problems," Treena said.

"My wife and I don't do that often enough," I told them. "Sometimes, I think, there's a feeling of self-consciousness."

"I believe you *must* pray together," Graham said. "All prayer needs a partner so that you can share answers to prayer. And God also acts as a mediator for us."

"We talk to the Father," continued Treena, "And we hear each other confessing our sins."

"Now and again, Treena's tongue language changes, becomes strident and compelling," Graham said. "At those times, I shut up and listen, and I sometimes get a kind of audio-video sequence. It's speaking and interpreting in tongues, and you usually need two people for that."

"What kind of interpretations are you talking about?" I asked, curious.

"For example, one time after Treena spoke in tongues, I found myself in the midst of this vision, wrapped all around me like 3-D television. I saw a camel with its head swaying back and forth. Then I saw the shoulder and then the main body, and a man sitting on the camel's back. On either side of the camel were long clay vessels, tied on with hemp around the saddle. The camel was walking down a narrow path toward an encampment, a little oasis.

"Then God began to speak to me: 'I'm just a purveyor of oil,' He said. 'I go from tent to tent, ladling out this oil—see how I do it? You'll see I take oil from one side, and then from

29

the other side. And I will replace the oil in a like amount in each vessel. You see, the camel is your marriage, and the vessels are you and your wife. The Holy Spirit is the oil. I will replace the Spirit regularly in you because if I didn't my camel would lose its balance and stumble in the path.'"

Treena, looking wistfully at Graham as he described his vision, said, "I have said, 'God, I want to have the interpretations of my tongues myself.' And God says, 'You've had them!' I say, 'I haven't!' And He says, 'What about Graham? Why do you need the interpretation when your husband has it?' We go through these stages when we feel one is being used more than the other. But God does work it out."

"Almost a subtle kind of competition again?" I asked, and they laughed.

"I envy and covet spiritual fruit, but we try not to envy and covet the gifts," Graham explained.

And so, as the Kerrs' spiritual adventure continued before my very eyes, I reluctantly got my things together and prepared to leave. Just before I departed, they invited me to pray with them and their secretary, Rita. We stood around in a circle, held hands, and prayed for some people they were concerned about. There were interjections of "Praise God!" and "Thank you, Jesus!" through the prayer. In almost a physical sense, I felt as though some huge, benevolent arm had reached out and embraced me—perhaps as a signal to let me know that the "Galloping Gourmet" clan had definitely accepted me into their spiritual family.

Chapter 3

# *On the Trail of God*

## NOEL PAUL STOOKEY

Peter, Paul, and Mary.

Remember the great songs they used to sing? "Puff (the Magic Dragon)" . . . "I Dig Rock and Roll Music" . . . Bob Dylan's "Blowin' in the Wind" and Pete Seeger's "Where Have All the Flowers Gone."

Their music spanned the counterculture decade of the 1960s. In many ways, they were *the* musical spokesmen for the sixties. But now, to paraphrase their popular song, "where have Peter, Paul and Mary gone?" Why did they decide to break up after such a successful ten years of concert tours and album sales? Did the split have anything to do with Paul's reported conversion to Christianity?

These questions were rattling around in my brain as I drove north through New England to visit Noel (Paul) Stookey at his country home in South Blue Hill, Maine. Of course, there were other thoughts in my mind too. I couldn't help but feel a slight yearning at Noel's ability to retire in his mid-thirties with an incredible accumulation of fame and fortune. I knew that at this stage of my life I wouldn't be happy giving up my work and running away to a rural setting. But still, I had toyed with a few ideas along those lines, and I was curious about comparing his actual experience with my own fantasies about escaping the city.

Noel's personality defies easy description. The terms "loose cat" and "Jesus freak" came to my mind when he informed me in a casual, handwritten note that he had set up a sound studio on the top floor of an old henhouse. After I arrived in South Blue Hill, I saw that the studio was, indeed, in an ex-henhouse. But the mental image I had of a dilapidated old coop, full of dirty, dank feathers and bird droppings, was quickly dispelled. Stookey had revamped both the exterior and interior and filled the studio with the latest sound equipment. When in operation, his control room was full of blinking, colored lights and whirling tapes, and reminded me of the latest NASA space module. His home was across the country road that ran in front of the studio, and he was remodeling the roof with metal solar reflectors as part of a solar energy system he expected to rely on heavily in the future. A meadow stretched out beyond his yard and ended on an expansive bay, which opened into the Atlantic Ocean. The scene was idyllic—just the sort of place where I'd always dreamed of doing my writing. And Noel Stookey, as it happened, was just the sort of person I'd like to have living next to me.

As we sat down to talk in some comfortable chairs in his sound studio, I realized he was much more than just a loose cat. The tall, balding folk singer followed my every comment and question with penetrating, soulful eyes, as though he was interested in me primarily as a human being, and not just an interviewer. His remarks, which drifted through a flowing, Zapata mustache, were incisive, thoughtful, and sometimes profoundly philosophical. And there was occasionally a touch of the humor that had made him the "comedy man" in the Peter, Paul and Mary trio.

I sensed at the beginning of our conversation that his conversion had radically altered his entire life, including his relationship with Peter and Mary. But I knew that to get the full picture, I'd have to start at the beginning of his spiritual quest.

"What's your earliest memory of Christianity?" I asked.

"My mom," he said simply. "But I went to church with her maybe only four or five Sundays in my childhood that I can recall."

"What's your real name—Noel or Paul?"

"My name is Noel Paul Stookey, but I changed my name to

adopt Paul as a middle name. I didn't want to change my first name as part of the Hollywood syndrome." But because "Paul" sounds better with "Peter" and "Mary," Noel decided to accommodate the demands of show business to some extent.

"Did you have any interest in music in your childhood?" I wondered.

"Oh, yes," Noel said, staring with a satisfied smile through a studio window at the woods and bay that stretch out below us. "My earliest recollection of being interested in music was seeing circuses that came through the town in Maryland where I grew up. Of course, I came from a very musical family. Dad had been a drummer; he played in a dance band. Mom was shy but had a sweet voice. We did a lot of traveling because Dad was on the road a lot, and we'd sing to pass the time. I learned to sing harmony and play a ukelele and began performing at age five or six in school assemblies."

Noel got more seriously involved in music during high school in Michigan and at Michigan State University. "If there was a show on campus, I was probably the M.C. of it. I also started to write my own songs and play the electric guitar."

But Noel was not particularly interested in the academic life, so he dropped out of college with a sophomore ranking and went to New York City. He wasn't intent on making his fortune but just had a whimsical interest in photography and decided to take a job as production manager for a chemical photography company.

"I was blessed by not having any ambition," he told me with a casual smile. "If anything came into my life that seemed fun, I'd do it. Most often, I never sought opportunities."

Instead, they just fell into his lap. I liked this style, but I could tell I might have some trouble understanding him since my own personality had been more influenced by a Protestant-ethic achievement orientation.

He mentioned that while he was in New York he landed a part-time job singing and entertaining in Greenwich Village, so I asked, "Do you think there was any inner drive, any career goal that drove you to begin singing in the Village?"

"No," he shrugged. "I started coming to Greenwich Village because I wanted to play chess."

"Chess?"

"Yes, there were a lot of chess players there, and I enjoyed it. Across the street from where I was playing was a coffee house called the Gaslight. I saw a stage there, and something prompted me to ask if they were looking for entertainment. The manager listened to me sing, and said, 'Okay, come on in on weekends.' Seems like that has happened all my life: I've done things that feel very natural, and I get paid for them."

"A lot of people would think that's a great position to be in!" I laughed.

"Strangely enough, I'd like to get out of that position now," he replied pensively. "I'd like to feel like I'm doing some honest labor, preferably physical labor. Not that the other was dishonest labor . . ."

"You mean you don't think you've been living under the curse of man in Genesis, working under the sweat of the brow?" I said, half-jokingly.

"Yes, that to me is labor. I'm being paid here for questions of judgment and taste," he said, gesturing at the equipment in his recording studio. "I provide film scores for shows on Maine public TV, and people come in off the street to record their demos [demonstration records]. I'm the engineer for them, but I'm not sweating when I get through the day. I was hopeful when I moved up here that as the snow thawed, so would my muscles."

As our conversation shifted back to the story of his performing career, I asked, "Did you consider yourself to be a Christian when you were singing and playing chess there in the Village?"

"Oh, no," he replied. "Well, that's not quite true. I suppose I would have *considered* myself to be one, but I didn't realize how personal a relationship I could have with Christ, how integral prayer could be in a person's life. I didn't know what the word 'Christian' really meant. To me, a Christian was a person who tried to do well, went to church, lived a good life." He thought for a moment and then added, "But you know, I've found that my style of life in those days was quite similar to the Christian style of life."

"You mean taking things as they come, without worrying too much about the future?" I asked.

He nodded, and I had to agree. "That's really true," I said.

34

"Trying to control life to the last detail is something a lot of Christians have to *un*learn. I find one of the hardest things for me is to rely completely on God and not attempt to plan my life ten years in advance. That kind of long-range planning never works anyhow, but in the past I felt a compulsion to *try* to control my future."

"Part of being a responsible man," Noel mused.

As his singing jobs increased, Noel said, he began to show up later and later for work at the photography company. Finally, he quit work and devoted full time to his performing. As his reputation grew, he was approached by Albert Grossman, "who was the Sol Hurok of what was beginning to bubble as folk entertainment," Noel said. "This was going to be my big chance. But he asked if I wanted to join a group. I thought, 'No, that isn't what you're supposed to say, Albert. You're supposed to ask me if I'd like a movie contract.' So I said no, I didn't want a group. I wanted to do some things by myself first before I got into that."

That encounter occurred in late 1959 or 1960, according to Noel. "I think now that the group he had in mind included Mary Travers and Peter Yarrow," he told me. "Mary lived in the Village and had been with Pete Seeger. She sometimes went over to Washington Square Park and sang her lungs out against people like the Clancy Brothers. Peter had been on tour and was actually better grounded in folk music than either Mary or myself. He had come to it academically—conducted a folk music course at Cornell. He not only could sing the Appalachian songs, but he also knew where they came from.

"Mary soon called me directly—I had worked out some songs for her on previous occasions. I knew her because she frequented the place where I performed. She said, 'There's a guy I'm with, and I'm wondering if we could get together and sing.'

"Well, somebody puts it like that, and I'm going to say no? So she came over with Peter and after discarding several songs we finally decided to sing 'Mary Had a Little Lamb.' It felt wonderful. There was an instinctive understanding of harmony. Peter has a beautiful tenor voice, I'm a baritone, and Mary is an alto—though if the intent is there, she can hit any note she wants to."

The three went to work immediately to prepare some songs, primarily to convince Albert Grossman that they sounded good enough to be booked somewhere. "Under Peter's aggressive leadership and ability to pull things together, we came up with three or four songs and sang them to Albert. He was sitting in a chair, just like you are," he said, nodding at the way I was relaxing in a big armchair. "We were nervous, but when we finished, he said, 'Well, that's it! If nothing happens, *you're* going to happen!' I guess he really liked us.

"Sure enough," he continued, "it just began to fall into place"—just like everything else in Noel's life, I thought. "We got a job as a group at a coffee house in the Village, but the only way they could afford to pay us was if we did all the entertainment."

"Did you just sing during your segment?" I asked.

"I did a comedy routine too," he said.

"What kind of stuff would you do? I mean, I can't imagine standing up in front of an audience and being funny."

"Really?" he replied, almost incredulous, as though *anyone* should be able to make an audience laugh.

"No, I can't imagine it," I said.

"I'm sure that you could easily make people laugh if you'd talk to them in a certain personal way."

"I can't tell a joke," I insisted.

"Well, I never told jokes either, but I'd reveal thoughts which an amazing number of other people apparently had thought, though they never admitted it to anyone. And to have this fellow on stage admitting such things . . ."

"Like what?" I asked.

"Sometimes I'd pick a common topic like smoking, and do a five-minute thing about what it meant to me. I smoked pretty heavily, two packs a day. It was an opportunity to try to expunge my own habit by speaking about it. I'd be smoking and begin to talk about what a cigarette meant. 'Why do you need a cigarette when you want it?' I might ask. 'Why do you need it after being under pressure? It's because you need security! Your cigarette is your mother. You know, contrary to popular belief, my friends in the Village and I are not going to package marijuana and sell it in stores. Instead, we're going to package pacifiers. Soon, it will be perfectly acceptable to see a man walking down the street with a ring hanging out of his mouth. Think of the money we'll make, with the silver chains and other accessories to go with pacifier sales!' "

Such routines became a regular part of the performance, and the group's structure gradually became formalized. Peter would come out by himself at the beginning of the second half of the program and sing with the audience. Then he would introduce Noel, who would do his act and finally introduce the entire group. They began to play on a supper club circuit across the country and also started to record their first albums for Warner Brothers in 1960 and 1961.

"I was young, giddy, flattered, self-centered, getting cocky," Noel remembered. "But I still was not motivated by ambition —not unless the collection of material objects is ambition. Nor was I motivated by betterment of status, or becoming the greatest singer in the world. I guess my main motivation was just fun, though it's not fair to pass through this era without commenting on our attitudes toward the social significance of what we were doing. The nature of our songs advised our audiences of the joy of being together, the sympathy we felt for those enduring hardships because of ignorance and injustice. It was the civil rights period, the age of social altruism. But the seeds of my disillusion were already there because what we hoped for in our hearts—a peaceful and loving country—was in fact not transpiring. It was the dilemma that every altruistic heart of the sixties began to encounter.

"Also, a personal paradox was developing in my life. Here I was, a boy who enjoyed life, who was open to most everything, who wanted to help people—but who at the same time had started to collect those material things he enjoyed."

"I guess it was inevitable that your altruism would disappear or atrophy unless you found something to give it firmer foundation," I commented.

"Yes," he agreed. "A contradiction has to occur at some point between altruism and material collection. As collection captures more and more of your interest, you make subtle sacrifices so that you can collect even more. And your soul begins to die. That was what was beginning to happen to me."

The group began to see "big money—the kind that would give me a collection of XKE's, a town house in New York, vacations in Barbados" by 1963, when their third album came out, he said. After Noel married his wife, Betty, in 1963, things seemed to get better and better for him. But in 1966, he entered a "real down period," he said. For one thing, he explained, "I got very heavy into marijuana. I began to write songs under the influence of pot—'I Dig Rock and Roll Music' and 'The House Song,' for example. I'd smoke every day, but I didn't realize at the time how subtly debilitating marijuana is. In the beginning, it relieved me of all restrictions that my mind or habits had placed on me. It was as though I could stand outside myself. When I was on marijuana, I was in two places at once."

"What motivated you to get into pot?" I wondered.

"That's kind of hard to pin down. Maybe a need to have a clearer understanding of reality. But it was relatively accessible in the Village—trying it then was like trying a can of beer, or a cigarette. It was available, and it was a lark—not to be taken seriously. It caused euphoria, was relatively inexpensive, and entailed no apparent penalty when you woke up the next morning. I sometimes smoked marijuana when I sat down to listen to the Beatles—this became almost a 'must' for listening critically to music. So I started smoking all the time. There seemed no reason not to because cost wasn't a factor. Up to 1966, things went well in every way—financially, emotionally. I was a happy person. Looking back through a Christian perspective, I'd say I had successively completed my own deification. I was a god to myself at that point, infallible, and maybe arrogant. In creating myself as a god, I had erected around myself tools of power—fame, plenty of money, a landmark house, a telephone in my car."

But thunderheads were already appearing on the horizon of Noel's life. "I was not very family-oriented, though I had a wonderful family," he said. "I traveled a lot and I became very selfish. I was becoming, if not an eccentric, at least outrageous. Even though we might have set up an evening to socialize, if I didn't want to go out, I wouldn't go. If I was supposed to go to a meeting, I might lie without much hesitation to get out of it. That's the fine, forked-tongued aspect of marijuana. It weakens your will power so you can do anything your desires would have you do. On the other hand, it endows you with impeccable insight, making you totally aware of what you've done. You're incredibly perceptive of your irresponsibility. Marijuana is very subtle—it gives you an ability not to care. But it's very difficult to advise early users about this because it has to reveal itself personally. So anyhow, I was becoming more and more selfish. And even though the group was still going forward successfully in 1966, I was beginning to flail about [without purpose]."

"There's an interesting point here," I remarked. "There was an emphasis in your songs on altruism, on global love and helping mankind in general, but somehow you weren't putting this love into practice on a personal level."

"That's exactly it," he agreed. "And I had a real thirst to make that love more specific, but we're not to that point yet. As I said, there was a clarity in my perception of myself, but at the same time a certain weakness in trying to exercise any will power. And that weakness was probably justified, because why on earth should I restrain myself? What was the value of will power? I had experienced almost everything fame and money could buy. I was succeeding in the world marketplace. But I realized that none of these achievements was making me happy internally."

So Noel embarked on a serious inner spiritual quest, a search to find the meaning of life. His questioning first led him to explore the timeless virtues, truth and love. "Truth emerged as an integral tool [in my search], a basic standard that at a certain level had to be inviolate. So here's this poor kid, Noel Stookey, deciding truth is where it's at. If he misses a meeting now, what's he going to do? He can't make up some cocka-mamy story, as he did in the past. Instead, he has to be completely honest and outspoken in saying, 'No.' Truth replaced kindness. It was tantamount to running up to some lady on the street and saying, 'That's a ridiculous hat!' Truth became a cause, and I immediately began to reveal it to as many people as I could find. But then I discovered truth was not the answer because I was just being truthful about my selfishness. It was a step in the right direction, but not the ultimate end I was seeking."

So instead of dwelling on truth, Noel moved on to love. "We always expected social altruism could be effected by putting the right people in the right political positions," he said. "It was a few misguided people who had gotten our society into such a mess. But then I began to replace this [social] cause with a new, more personal cause called love. I didn't know a lot about love, but it seemed if more people were in love, we'd have less problems. I was beginning to see the wisdom of caring for your immediate neighbor. But I was still in a twilight zone, looking for real values."

Dissatisfied with the results of his search for truth and love, Noel decided to travel to Woodstock, New York, to talk over things with his friend, songwriter Bob Dylan. "I knew him in the Village," he told me. "We made him popular, but it would have been just a matter of time. 'Blowin' in the Wind' was his first big entrance into American consciousness."

Sitting down next to Dylan, who was just recovering from a motorcycle accident, Noel said, "Okay, Bob, all around me, on radio, I hear that love is the answer. You've always been into the right things—how come your albums don't reflect that?"

In fact, Noel was probing to find whether Dylan had discovered the answers to the philosophical questions he himself was asking. But Dylan never answered him directly. "He always said, 'Where do *you* think it's at?'" Noel told me. "I said, 'The music that's coming out now is talking about a kind of answer that is relevant to living on a day-to-day basis, not to politics. Where are you at now?' He said, 'I'm working on an album now. You'll hear it soon, and I think you'll like it.' It was *John Wesley Harding* and it had spiritual overtones, but I'm still not sure I understand it."

Though most of Dylan's responses were rather indirect or indefinite, he did offer two helpful pieces of advice, Noel said. "You're from the Middle West—will you be going back there soon?" Dylan asked him. "Well, the first thing you should do is go back there and walk about. And the second thing you should do is read the Bible."

Now, Noel had some direction. And he acknowledges that Dylan's first suggestion—returning to his boyhood haunts—"was a knockout! By going back to Michigan where I had gone to college, where I had wasted three years, I suddenly realized I had been a slave to myself in those days. I didn't want education and didn't take advantage of what was available because I was looking for things to please or appease me. I was already making compromises in terms of peer approval. I preferred popularity to grades." These early experiences had apparently set a pattern that had influenced his later life.

As for Dylan's advice about the Bible, "I could make no sense of it," Noel admitted. "But I had a lot of respect for him, as I did for anybody who spoke the truth. If truth was involved, I'd have walked into hell with him to perceive what he was perceiving."

"So did you start to read the Bible?" I wondered.

"Sure," he said with a grin.

"What part of the Bible?"

"Right at the beginning—isn't that where you're supposed to start with any book? And it made no sense. I could not apply it to my life. It was six months later that somebody finally told me to start at the New Testament. I understand now that Christ was the culmination of those things I was reading in the Old Testament. He's the key to unlock the Old Testament."

"Who told you that?" I asked.

"I think it was a Spirit-filled ex-disk jockey named Scott Ross," he replied. "He was a witness to me and spoke of his faith, but I wasn't interested at the time. He seemed to have committed himself to something in another world, and I was still looking for solutions in this world."

During the months that followed, Noel was "on the trail of God," he said. He pursued every possible line of inquiry, "except personal prayer." He even met the Episcopal bishop, Paul Moore, Jr., who then lived in Washington, D.C. "He invited me into his study and talked to me for a half hour," the singer said. "I don't remember coming to any conclusion, but I was just gratified that he had heard me out. I know the effect of intercession, and I'm sure he prayed for me."

Then came the most fateful day of his life—a Peter, Paul and Mary concert in Austin, Texas.

The group had been playing before a big crowd, perhaps twelve thousand people, and Noel was tired when he walked backstage during the intermission. When Peter went on to start the second half of the concert, Noel stayed behind to tune his guitar, and a teenaged boy approached him as he was working on his instrument. The boy introduced himself as Steve Hance and said he wanted to talk, but Noel hesitated.

"It was an awkward moment," Noel told me, "because I had to be onstage in a few seconds. But I was just beginning to realize how important it is to love people, and I wanted to try to live by that conviction. I wanted to give love, even though I didn't know how to get it. 'Maybe it has to start here,' I thought to myself. I was an agnostic then—at least I didn't believe in a God who touched people personally. I was ready to do a solo of a song I'd written, 'Love City (Post Cards to Duluth),' which had a line that said, 'Hey, Margaret, I left you a note . . . did you get what I wrote . . . I laid it between your records . . .' That was in effect to say that every song I've written is an attempt to communicate with people. 'Margaret' represents Middle America to me.

"I thought this Steve, like most kids, was going to tell me some of his problems, to which I would reply with some advice. He was sad, almost morose."

So Noel replied to Steve, "I'll look for you when I come off the stage after the concert." When Noel saw Steve later that evening, he walked over and put an arm on his shoulder. He sensed something was troubling the boy, a burden of some sort.

"What do you want to talk about?" Noel asked.

"I want to talk to you about the Lord," Steve replied.

Noel, in recounting this incident, told me he had a feeling "that this was it. The time had come. I was going to get zapped. It was a physical feeling, with my heart beating and adrenalin pumping. Something critical and unknown was going to happen. Steve began talking to me backstage even as I was signing autographs, and I became completely focused on what he was saying, almost as though the other people weren't there. He was talking about how he had been on an acid trip with two other friends in an automobile. It had been a bad trip, but he began praying in the name of Jesus. He said he had immediately become straight—his consciousness was altered back to normal. I knew that was impossible."

"I've heard of that happening in other people," I said.

"Through prayer?" Noel asked.

"Yes."

"I have too, now, but this was the first time I'd ever heard of such a thing. I thought it was impossible. On the other hand, I knew Steve was a person who spoke the truth. I said, 'I know it's happened to you because you speak with conviction.' There was no sense this kid was a kook. He went on to tell me that, little by little, it was revealed to him and his friends that prayer was the only way, and if they called on Jesus' name, they would receive what they needed. So they became Jesus freaks."

The conversation between Noel and Steve finally became so intense that Steve suggested, "Can we go someplace that's more private to talk?" Although Noel would usually have refused to commit any more of his time to one young person, he knew he couldn't deny this request. So he invited Steve and one of Steve's companions to the motel room where he was staying. But Noel found himself trying to divert the conversation from Christ whenever possible. "As we got into a pickup truck and drove toward my motel, I hit Steve with the heaviest piece of spiritual information I had: 'Do you believe in spiritual reincarnation?' I asked. He replied, 'It may or may not be true, but it seems there are more important things to talk about.' I thought, 'More important than reincarnation? How can that be?'

"When we got back to the motel, I did everything I could to change the subject, to make the evening lighter, to try to get rid of the load. I turned the air conditioner on, offered 7-Ups, tried to refract the experience. I couldn't handle it in one large chunk. But they would have none of it. When that motel door closed, Steve said, 'I think we should pray.' I had never prayed in the past except in really pressing situations. You know, 'God get me out of this mess.' I had enough belief during those moments of duress to call on the most significant thing I had in my forgiveness arsenal—which was God.

"But Steve was engaging in active prayer as a dialogue. This was totally new to me. He was obviously operating from a different resource than I was aware of, and the 7-Ups I offered had no relationship to his motives for being there."

According to Noel, they all knelt on the floor, and Steve prayed, "Father, I want to thank You for getting me into the concert tonight and placing the burden on me to talk to Paul. I thank You for getting me past the guards with no ticket. You know what a burden I've had on my heart for Paul. Now, Noel wants to talk to You."

Steve then stood up and walked over and laid his hands on Noel's head. Noel's first reaction was that it would be phony for him to say anything, but when he finally did begin to speak, he started to cry. He said, "Lord, forgive me . . ." and then, between sobs, he sighed, "Phew!" to try to control his emotions.

Although Noel's memory of his exact prayer is hazy, he told me, "I think I mentioned I had denied God in one way or another. I never said, 'Take over my life' at that point, but I think I became a Christian then."

"It was a decision on your part, a kind of repentance and commitment?" I asked.

"Yes. I felt that I was letting go and letting, or admitting, God. It may sound presumptuous, but it was as though I was issuing an invitation to God. I believe Christ dwelled inside me at that point. Steve came back the next morning with his girlfriend, and we had breakfast together. I felt like a new person. My life had taken a turn. It was like, 'Hey! I made a commitment, the biggest commitment in the world!' I didn't understand what it all involved then, what the potential was, but I prayed incessantly. Initially, I didn't know how to pray, but it was really the Spirit showing me how. I started doing things, which I didn't understand, but, in retrospect now, I know they were right. For example, I'd go into situations and just pray and ask God, 'Where should I go? Take this elevator? Sit down next to this man?' The loose structure of living I'd developed on the road fit easily into this loose Christian life-style."

Noel now does some of his most effective praying—as both Graham Kerr and I do—in his morning shower. "I didn't really learn what prayer was until I read the book *Instrument of Thy Peace* by Alan Patton," he said. "To be an instrument of God's peace seems a more proper attitude in prayer—less selfish and more 'Thy will be done.' Most people who express disbelief or disappointment in prayer are praying selfishly. They're praying that God will bend a few natural laws to hand them what they want. But it takes a while to learn that you have to submit to His will to get what is right for your life."

His words reminded me of what the Apostle James said of prayer in James 4:3: "You ask and do not receive, because you ask wrongly, to spend it on your passions." As Noel talked about his increased desire to establish a firm relationship with

God through prayer, I wondered what was happening to his relationship with the people around him. Specifically, did his new faith inject tensions into the singing group?

"There was always a section of the program where we talked about those things that were relevant to us," he said. "Well, what was relevant to me now? It became my witness, though I still used funny lines and jokes. This led to a series of arguments, and eventually came to a head in a discussion one night during the halftime of one of our concerts. Peter was onstage, and Mary and I got to talking. It wasn't the first time Mary had expressed the feeling of being upset because she said her friends came in to see her at a concert and had to endure my witnessing. I said, 'Well, when the group first got together, we didn't have any structure. We evolved out of what we naturally felt was a nice way to relate to a bunch of people.' But Mary said she believed Peter, Paul and Mary were not art any more. We had crossed over that threshold of taste and art, she said, into something approaching a Southern Baptist revival meeting. That was an exaggeration, but I usually allowed for exaggeration. I said, 'Well, I hadn't realized what an incredible parallel there was between Frank Lloyd Wright's form-follows-function and what I am about to say, but we never designed what we became. The fact that some people want to call us art is their prerogative, but the art came as a description of what we did naturally.' "

Noel summed up his reaction to Mary's objections this way: "For the first time, I was to be edited or censored, even though I had *never* been censored talking about [things like] marijuana."

Such censorship of his new Christian convictions was unacceptable to Noel. At the same time, other problems started cropping up. There seemed to be a growing feeling that the original impetus that drove the group to sing about social progress and togetherness was abating. "We had [sensed] a definite calling," Noel said. "The three of us had felt we were making a definite contribution. We didn't know exactly what we were sharing, but we felt our popularity was not a result of mere showmanship. It was real, had substance to it. It had something to do with love, something to do with believing what we sang.

"But at an antiwar moratorium rally in about 1969, I found I

45

was perceiving the moratorium through different eyes because I had become a Christian. I now perceived life as one-to-one, not as politics and moving masses of people. It was nice that a large group of people could come together, but I knew now that the person who put the microphone on the stage was just as important as the person who was about to sing. I realized that no one was more important than the person you were next to. I sensed the focus of our group had become refracted. There was no such thing as the liberal point of view any more. And it wasn't enough just to be opposed to certain issues, like the war. I could feel things breaking up because of the way popular music was going. In the late sixties popular music changed from songs that spoke of togetherness to those that spoke of one-to-one relationships. The Woodstock festival was an expression of this new kind of music."

Noel's concern as a Christian to improve his personal relationships naturally caused him to take a closer look at his family situation. After that, the break-up of the group was inevitable. "I felt my primary ministry had to be with my family," Noel said. "It would have been no good, empty, to go out on the road for a great length of time, talking about how I had found happiness through Christianity, and at home have a cesspool of neglect. I'd go out on the road with the group, sing songs about the sunrise, country mornings, altruistic love—and still have my meals sent up by room service and never see the sunrise because we'd sleep until 2 P.M. I wanted to live life coherently, consistently with the faith, so that when I got up on a stage, my performance would be an extension of who I really was."

"So you told Peter and Mary you wanted to leave the group?" I asked.

"It was my decision to say I'm not going to travel," he said. " 'If you want to make records,' I said, 'that's okay.' This was in Japan, maybe in 1970. We had a couple of months of vacation coming up, and it was a good time to do it."

"Did the others offer any resistance?"

"How could there be resistance?" Noel replied. "We had a couple of steadfast rules. If one of us did not like a song, we didn't do it. It was minority rule. Sometimes, in the last couple of years, if somebody didn't want to do something and the other two did, those two would do it. It became less important to work as a group, more important to work as individuals in concerts."

Although Peter, Paul and Mary suspended operations as a group, Noel kept in touch with the other two—especially with Peter. "Peter had begun his own quest around the same time I did. His song-writing reflected that search. When you write songs, it's like anything creative: it involves a set of personal guideposts, a statement of self. You're trying to say something true and right."

Noel didn't want to disclose many details because of the confidential personal relationship that he and Peter still enjoy, but he did give one poignant example of how close they had remained after Noel's conversion. "Peter asked me to write a song for his wedding. The song—'Wedding Song (There Is Love)'—came as an answer to prayer, so I didn't feel right about putting my name on it as the author. I felt Jesus should be at Peter's wedding, not me singing 'moon, June, spoon.' I wanted Peter to understand the significance of life, and I thought Christ and the Holy Spirit could do it best.

"Peter was overwhelmed," Noel said quietly. "It was a beautiful song, and God guided me, absolutely. It also became a top thirty single, and was the reason the album *Paul And* was so successful."

I had heard the song frequently on the radio and had always enjoyed it, but I'd never really paid close attention to the words. As I listened to an album Noel had given me, I could see for the first time how the words of Jesus in the Gospels (e.g., Matthew 18:20) pervaded the lyrics:

"He is now to be among you, at the calling of your hearts. Rest assured, this troubador is acting on His part. The union of your spirits here has caused Him to remain, for whenever two or more of you are gathered in His name, there is love, there is love" (Public Domain Foundation Inc., ASCAP).

As we relaxed in his studio and sipped cups of coffee, I became more aware of the quietness of the country, the clean air and bright sunshine. "You know, your life up here is like one of my fantasies come to life," I confessed. "But for me, it might be more an escape than anything else. Is this a dream you've always had in the back of your mind, to live in an area like this? Or did you feel God leading you here?"

He thought for a moment, then replied, "Yes, I'd say I felt led. Insofar as I feel closer to God up here, yes, I feel I was led."

But Noel also said that he felt the country life would be good for his family relationships. "I guess I was looking for assistance from the environment, and we got none of that in the suburbs," he explained. "Our house in Rye [New York] was too large, and I wanted to get down to essences. We began looking for a country place about three years ago, a place to farm, where the kids could get lost in the woods. In Rye, we had an acre and a half, in a very spread-out suburban area. It was a very grand house with thirty rooms, a recording studio, a swimming pool. Too high on the hog, too rich for me. Betty still misses it, but I felt it was wasteful. The taxes cost less here. Our fuel bill is forty-nine dollars a month at this house, compared with two hundred a month in Rye."

But an even deeper theological reason underlay Noel's decision to head for the woods. He believes strongly that the prophecies in the Book of Revelation about the last days of history are coming to pass, and he wants to be prepared. "I have a sense that is based more on history than on premonition," he emphasizes. "When I read Revelation, I look to history as it is unfolding today to get a sense of when these things will come to pass. I figure it's just beyond my lifetime."

Noel is referring specifically to Revelation 13:11–18, which some Bible interpreters say predicts a dictator who will control the world's economy by requiring everyone to have a certain number tattooed on his forehead or right hand in order to buy and sell goods. The singer's response to this prophecy is to try to become self-sufficient economically so that his family and anyone else who may rely on them won't be subject to the future dictator's restrictions.

Noel has even written a song called "Miracles" which speaks of present tendencies toward control of the economy: "In the cold white light of the office, behind the security guard . . . the computer supplies suggestions to improve the credit card. The new card will be issued at the time of birth, and the credit potential will be determined for everyone on earth . . . and for

48

ease of identification, though there is some aversion now, the credit number will be tattooed on the wrist or on the brow. And so we build a beast revealed by miracles as time unfolds the prophets' dream. Remember what they say about coincidence . . . life is always more than it seems."

"There are, in fact, investigations by the Rand Corporation to improve the credit card," Noel said. "Of course, everyone has a Social Security number, and I have an article up there, on my bulletin board, that says a national identification card is on the drawing board."

Even if the last days are near—and I'm always reluctant to engage in predictions myself—I was not convinced that Noel's solution of returning to the land and becoming self-sufficient through farming is what God wants for all Christians. But I'll have to admit, as I sit in my smog-bound Manhattan office, that his approach is certainly one of the most enjoyable.

Pondering his immediate future, Noel pointed across the road to his home on the bay and said, "There's a greenhouse behind my house, and I'm not sure but that in ten or fifteen years it will be more important for me to be over there, tending crops in just the same way that farmers have for time immemorial. I have a real interest in beet and potato planting. This past year was our first year for a garden of decent size, and the first year I ever drove a tractor." He smiled a smile of deep satisfaction. "We got enough beans and potatoes, but we made a lot of mistakes. The corn never came in.

"I haven't written a song for a long time, so I think something else may be happening in that area. It may be that a phase of my life has passed. I still enjoy entertaining, singing, making people laugh, and I feel not enough people are doing it. Most of the entertainment nowadays doesn't seem concerned with the audience. The entertainers seem to remain apart from the audience. But I don't pray about my career—unless it's for some immediate inspiration. Of all the peace God has given me, the kind I'm most happy about is what transpires during a performance. If I can stay out of the way, my entire program is laid out for me. I avoid trying to overplan, or thinking too far ahead, or interjecting thoughts. I just do it as the Spirit moves me.

"I'm not sure but what my attitude toward my career is a result of having had a large success, both monetarily and publicly. I'm less inclined to worry about such things. As corny as it sounds, I didn't go out and look for my success in show business. I got plucked, placed, and profited. When kids call me and ask, 'What should I do?' I usually just look into myself and say, 'Believe in what you're doing, love it, don't look for payment. That's all I can tell you.'

"Of course, when something falls through, I say to myself, 'I'm going to have to dig in someplace and get some kind of security together.' That's not unusual. I don't see how you can go through life without being anxious at one time or another—unless you're born and conceived of the Spirit."

Then he turned again to what seems to be his fondest interest, his new role as a country farmer. "Living here has a continuity of time that you can't find anywhere but in the country," he said, whetting my appetite still further for this quiet, healthy way of life. "There's no hurry. You could drive by that field out there last year, and there would have been nothing. Six months later, there would be a couple of stones. Six months after that, some more stones and a few blocks of wood. Three more months, and there might be a stake in the ground. People here are content to do things in small steps, and then wait and rest. There's a patience that is inherent in country living. I sometimes think in terms of putting a rat in a box or maze, and letting him find his way quietly to the end. And in another box, I imagine the same rat in the same maze, except that at about eighty-five decibels you play records, fire gunshots, sound police sirens. I guess they would both make it to the end of the maze, but there's a difference in style. I felt there was something I could learn from the country that I would not learn from the city."

He pondered for a moment, then concluded, "I feel God made the country, but I don't know who made the city."

I drove away from South Blue Hill with those words echoing in my mind, and with a nagging urge to abandon the urban hassle and move to the country myself—provided I could find a neighbor like Noel Paul Stookey.

50

# Chapter 4

# *Comebacks with Christ*
## TED PLUMB AND
## DENNIS RALSTON

Professional sports teams, with all their attendant publicity, present some of the most dramatic opportunities to reach the loftiest heights of achievement and acclaim. But chance injuries or a losing streak can plunge any star player to the lowest depths of failure and force him to fall back on his inner resources as he tries to pick up the pieces of his life.

The importance of such spiritual strength particularly impressed me as I talked with Ted Plumb, assistant coach of the New York Giants professional football team. An acquaintance from the Fellowship of Christian Athletes told me I should get in touch with Ted because "he's a man who doesn't just talk—he really *lives* his faith." I realized how true those words were as I listened to the quiet, modest Ted describe his own amazing spiritual comeback.

"I accepted the Lord when I was twelve," he began after we sat down in an office at the Giants' headquarters in Pleasantville, New York. "I had been longing and searching for God as I listened to people in Bible studies and church groups talk about things that were everlasting. I wrestled with these eternal issues and decided, yes, Somebody *has* died for my sins, so I finally made a public profession of faith at our Presbyterian church. It wasn't a bolt of lightning with me, but just a quiet

51

thing. I remember my mother saying she had prayed for me, and I know there was a great deal of home influence."

As it happened, it was crucially important for young Ted to have a strong spiritual underpinning for his life at that point because just a few months later his father committed suicide. "My faith helped me a great deal with that," he recalled solemnly. "There was an inner strength that helped the entire family during the next few years. I had two older sisters, and financially we were in a tough situation. My mother hadn't much experience with work, and she only had a couple of years of college, so she had to go on and get an education—a master's degree, eventually. She got some small Social Security benefits for widows, and that helped pay a few bills, but there was no sense my world had collapsed. We had a loving, giving family situation, and my faith in Christ made me just know we were going to be provided for. I didn't know how, but I was confident God would help us."

The spiritual growth that Ted experienced in those early years convinced him that God would never test him so severely that he would be tempted to give up his faith, rather than seek God's will. Paul's words in 1 Corinthians 10:13 became a living reality in his life: "No temptation has overtaken you that is not common to man. God is faithful, and he will not let you be tempted beyond your strength, but with the temptation will also provide the way of escape, that you may be able to endure it." Little did Ted realize how important this Christian principle would become as he moved inexorably toward another, and perhaps the most devastating personal challenge of his life.

Ted Plumb had wanted to be a football player almost from birth. He remembers telling his mother in the fourth grade, "You *have* to promise me, Mom, that you'll let me play football!" She promised, and Ted immediately proceeded to outstrip all his competitors in high school and junior college. He went on to become a split end for Baylor University and played in a couple of bowl games before he graduated in 1962.

"When I got out of college, I wanted to shoot for one of my lifelong goals," he reminisced. "I wanted to play pro ball. I wanted to give it a whirl so I wouldn't be saying through my life, 'I wish I would have done this, I wish I would have tried it.' I decided I was going to satisfy that hunger and find out if I was good enough. If not, I had always wanted to get into coaching, so I'd try that instead.

"I went to Buffalo to try out for the Bills as a free agent. They had a position open, and I felt like I had a chance to make it, especially after they didn't cut me."

But then disaster struck. During a practice session, Ted went up for a pass and was tackled, hard. "I dove for the ball, and the defense guy drove me into the ground. Instead of bellying into the ground and sliding along on my stomach, or doing a somersault, I was driven into the ground like a javelin, head-first. I didn't fully realize how badly I was hurt at the time, so I got off the ground and tried to walk away. But my hands were going numb, and I started crying and couldn't quit. I went to the trainer and said, 'I don't know what's the matter, but I can't quit crying. I don't know what's the matter with me.' I went to the hospital on a stretcher, with my head held in place by sandbags. My neck was broken, and some ribs were torn loose from my sternum."

As he was undergoing treatment at the hospital, his doctor told him, "You can play again if you want to, and we'll know if you're recovered if you take another heavy lick and it severs your spinal column." Ted got the message. If he decided to go onto the football field again, he might well be paralyzed for life or even killed.

"So, I guess you felt pretty low after hearing that?" I asked.

"Low! You're talking about not only losing a golden opportunity, but an entire career!" he exclaimed. "It was gone! Everything I had pointed toward since the fourth grade came to a screeching halt. I was probably in the best physical condition of my life then. I wanted to play a few years, get a little nest egg, and then get into coaching. I had always felt that God could communicate through me as a coach, but I had wanted to postpone it for a few years. That was the low point of my life, and I found myself questioning whether I really believed. I did a great deal of praying and questioning: 'Why me? Why now? Why at this point?' I went through a real heavy depression."

But then God began to answer his prayers after a couple of weeks, and the previous years, during which he had been developing spiritual muscle, helped him to recover inside, just as his body was healing on the outside.

53

"He gave me strength and showed me it isn't my right to question why," Ted said. "And He helped me recall, 'Hey, remember you always wanted to get out and influence people in coaching? Well, here's your opportunity.'"

Once again, God had made good on His promise in 1 Corinthians 10:13 and had not tested Ted beyond his spiritual strength. When Ted accepted coaching as God's plan for him and began actively looking for jobs, they fell into his lap in a way that would make many members of the coaching profession gasp in disbelief.

"Coaching is somewhat unique in that you don't go to an unemployment line and say, 'I want to coach,'" Ted said. "It's especially hard to get into pro coaching because there are so few open jobs."

He immediately landed a job as an assistant high school coach, quickly moved up to the junior college level, and then landed a position as an assistant coach on the staff of Texas Christian University. "Now, an opportunity to coach in college —many coaches coach a lifetime to get that opportunity," Ted said. "When I called up about the job, I thought I'd need a long list of high-powered names, but I had been recommended by another Christian coach. The coach I was talking to said, 'Don't worry about it,' and I went in three weeks later, and the job was mine."

Ted believes that the ease with which he secured these coaching jobs was entirely God's doing and not his own. He believes the same spiritual power was at work when he received a call from a New York Giants coach one evening as he was preparing to go out to a meeting of the Fellowship of Christian Athletes.

"Why don't you come up here and coach?" this Giants coach asked.

"Fine, and how's the weather?" Ted replied flippantly.

"No, why don't you?" the man insisted.

"Are you serious?" Ted asked.

"I'm serious."

So Ted Plumb and his family headed for New York, and his dream of pro football was fulfilled—but in a somewhat different way than he had expected. He has set up a Bible study for the Giants players and, in addition to his regular duties as coach of the receivers, he makes himself available to discuss spiritual and other personal problems with his players. His comeback from the depths of personal despair and physical disaster would probably have been impossible without that firm faith that began to grow at age twelve. And the impact of his ministry as a servant of Christ speaks for itself in the lives that are being influenced on the professional playing fields.

I witnessed firsthand a somewhat different kind of athletic comeback at the Spectrum in Philadelphia, during the 1976 U. S. Pro Indoor tennis tournament. Dennis Ralston and Australian star Rod Laver were pitted against Australians Ross Case and Geoff Masters, a highly successful doubles team who went on to the finals of the Wimbledon doubles championships later that year. Ralston and Laver had never played together before and were unseeded in the tournament.

My stomach was in knots as Ralston went back for an overhead smash, because somehow I sensed he was nervous. But he hesitated only slightly as he allowed the short lob to bounce above his head and then quickly crushed the ball into the far corner of the court for a winner.

Despite a busy schedule, which involved playing a packed singles and doubles schedule and taking some time off to speak at a presidential prayer breakfast, Ralston had agreed to share his Christian faith with me in Philadelphia. I had a personal interest in seeing him win because, for one thing, I had liked him from the moment we met. Also, I was sympathetic because I was aware of some of the factors that would likely make Dennis more nervous than the other players on the court.

I've been interested in tennis as an off-again, on-again player since I lettered on my high school doubles team in Dallas. Dennis Ralston and I are approximately the same age, and I used to read about how he was winning national and international competition as I was trying to struggle past first-round matches in local tournaments. We were in completely different leagues as tennis players. But I knew enough about the pressures of the game to sense to some extent what he was going through as I watched him lunge for volleys and throw his six-foot-three frame into powerful cross-court drives.

Ralston had particular reason to be jumpy that afternoon in

Philadelphia because he was in the process of trying to make a comeback, trying to regain confidence in himself after hitting a professional rock-bottom. He had been the great American hope in the mid-1960s—"the next Jack Kramer," according to some tennis pundits. He was ranked as number one male U.S. singles player for three straight years, won the Forest Hills doubles championship for three years, and won the Wimbledon doubles title as a teenager. In general, he seemed on the verge of grasping the world of tennis in the palm of his hand.

But then things started to go wrong. He began to lose key matches and developed a reputation as a tennis "bad boy." In fact, one man who was watching him warm up at the Spectrum said, "Didn't that guy used to be the Ilie Nastase of his day?"

"I seldom threw my racket, but I did knock some balls out of stadiums," Dennis admitted to me. "I'd get angry, that's for sure. Also, when I concentrate, I knit my brows and scowl, and that makes people think I'm glowering and angrier than I am."

It's a matter of record that Ralston was suspended at a Davis Cup match in Cleveland in the early 1960s for allegedly swearing and insulting Mexican Davis Cup captain Pancho Contreras. Ralston has told the press that he first swore at himself after slipping on a wet spot on the court and then refused Contreras' offer of a towel (*Tennis* magazine, February 1976, pages 34–35).

Things seemed to go from bad to worse. Dennis developed a degenerative knee condition in 1968, which hurt his performance. His playing ended altogether in 1972 when he was laid up with appendicitis for six weeks and then tore a cartilage in his knee. He did retain a position of great prestige in American Tennis by continuing as the nonplaying Davis Cup captain. But when his teams lost three straight years in early-round matches and the world's number-one singles player, Jimmy Connors, refused to play for him, he was fired.

So as I watched Ralston on the court in Philadelphia, I knew he had a great deal on his mind. At first, he glowered constantly—that concentration again—and his entire body seemed particularly tense. But then as the match swung clearly in his and Laver's favor, there were more smiles on Dennis's face. Laver and Ralston won 6–2, 7–6, and youthful autograph-seekers mobbed Dennis as he walked toward the locker rooms.

As we stretched out in our chairs later in his hotel room, he moved easily into a discussion of his faith: "I always felt there was a God, but I had no personal relationship with Him. When Linda and I first got married, she traveled with me a great deal, but by the mid-1960s, I had to be gone from home ten months out of the year and my attitude toward people got lousier. I didn't like the circuit. I didn't like the life-style, the things I was doing, the way I was playing. I didn't like myself nor did I think tennis was worth while. Boy, did it ever seem hollow! I knew something was missing, but I didn't know what it was. Linda and I were getting along, but she wasn't happy with herself either."

But then a decisive change occurred in their lives when Linda became a Christian in the summer of 1972. "I think God led her to be a Christian, in part so that I would be led into it," he mused. "I was gone on a Davis Cup trip at the time, and she started going to a Mennonite Brethren church in Bakersfield, California, where we live. When I came home, I recognized a big change in her and in her attitude toward me. 'I've taken the kids to church, and I'd like for you to go too,' she said. I didn't want to go, but I talked to the pastor and knew I was missing something. I felt guilty about my life-style and had even thought about quitting and opening up a gas station. My attitude affected the way I played tennis because I wasn't really concerned about how well I did."

Dennis finally gave in and started going to church himself. "That church was alive, and I really felt the people loved me and were warm toward me," he recalled. "They cared for me, and I needed that."

He also began to engage in deep spiritual conversations with American tennis star Stan Smith. "I knew he was a Christian with a strong faith," Dennis said. "I knew he had something, but I still didn't know how to go about getting it. I'd pray, but I guess I didn't give the right prayer. Then I read Hal Lindsey's book, *The Late Great Planet Earth,* as well as other Christian books, and I began to think maybe there is a Savior floating around in this world."

Ralston's spiritual crisis came to a head when, as the nonplaying captain, he took the U. S. Davis Cup team to Romania for the championship challenge round. "We were the defending champions and we had the choice of where the matches would be played, but Romania insisted we play in Romania, so we did. Nobody felt we had a chance to win there. Ilie Nastase and Ion Tiriac were playing against us. Tiriac, you know, wears a Fu Manchu mustache and is a really tough competitor. Their attitude is that they'll do anything to win. I wanted to be under control so that our guys would have more confidence in me."

While in Romania, Dennis approached Stan Smith, who was scheduled to play the key singles matches, and broached the questions that were still bothering him about Christianity: "Who is saved? How do you get saved? What about people who never heard about Christ? Was there really a creation?"

"They were all standard questions which Satan throws up as roadblocks," Dennis noted. "They still sometimes crop up in my mind because I'm a baby Christian, so to speak. But I had a lot of time to think because we couldn't leave the hotel. There had been Black September [terrorist] threats because we had two Jewish guys on the team, so we weren't free to move around."

As the matches began, Dennis prayed, "Lord, give me the strength not to lose my cool, my temper." He also recalls that he and Stan prayed together at the hotel, "though we never prayed for victory," he said.

"Smith won his matches under the most adverse conditions," Dennis said. "I don't think any other player could have won. The final score was 3–2 in our favor. I did get mad once when Tiriac was carrying on. [I thought] he had cheated Tom Gorman, so I called him a name. I was holding a racket, and would have decked him with it, but he walked around me."

Dennis acknowledges it was fortunate—or perhaps Providential—that Tiriac didn't take up his challenge because "there were four thousand Romanians and four of us. I've never been in a fight on the court, but I was ready that time."

When Dennis returned home to Bakersfield after this victory, he immediately went to church and tried to overcome the doubts that had been bothering him. At one service he heard a man speak who "was an evangelist, a hellfire and brimstone preacher. I had believed in God in Romania. And I had prayed in private, asking that Christ would come into my life, though I didn't know whether He would or had. This man, this evangelist, cleared up some of the dilemmas that were still bothering me. He reinforced my commitment, made me believe I had really been forgiven for my sins, no matter what I'd done. He said, 'You'll sin even if you're a Christian, but if you've made an effort, it will be all right.'"

As it happened, Dennis's main problem had been one that keeps many people from becoming Christians: he thought he had to clean up his own life completely first—work his way into heaven, so to speak—before God would accept him. "But this preacher showed me God would accept me *as I was,*" Dennis said. "He showed me how to take myself off the throne of my life and turn my problems over to God. I thought I had to live up to certain spiritual and moral standards. Only then, I thought, would God come in and lead me in spiritual growth. I thought I had to be perfect, and I didn't think I could be. But then I learned it wasn't required that I be perfect."

So Dennis was finally able to relax in his relationship with Christ, to accept the fact that God accepted him with all his human flaws and imperfections. I wondered, "Do you ever find yourself slipping back into doubts about your relationship with God?"

"Yes, and I'd venture that a lot of people have the same problem," he replied. "The main thing that helps me is to remember what Jesus said: 'Ask and you'll receive, knock and it will be opened to you.' When I start questioning, I go back to that."

"I find memorizing specific Bible verses like that one to be helpful in my own life," I told him. "As often as I can, I try to memorize just one short passage and then meditate on it. I find it sticks with me as I'm walking around, and when I confront a problem, God often seems to bring one of those verses to my mind to help me remember His promises and to give me resources to cope with different situations."

"That's a good thing to remember," he agreed.

"Today on the court you were smiling toward the end of the match, but sometimes you seemed to get annoyed, especially when you made an error," I noted. "Do you still use profanity in those situations?"

"I don't swear," he said. "Even in the old days, I didn't

swear a lot, though I occasionally used profanity. When you go into the locker room today, you can't believe the language," he remarked, shaking his head.

"But I remember you double-faulted once at a crucial time," I said. "I think I might have muttered something to myself in that situation—how do you hold it in?"

"If I let things like that bother me, it would affect the rest of my game," Dennis replied. "I know for me to play well, I have to be relaxed. I'm really churning every match I play now. But this gets back to my Christian experience. I prayed today, and it helped me get rid of my nervousness. I was playing well, but I was worried about my service, which had been giving me some problems. So I prayed, 'Lord, give me the strength to be relaxed, to play up to my ability. Help me just to play and not worry what happens. Help me not to choke.'" He smiled and, glancing at his ailing knee, said, "I'm just thankful that I'm out there able to play. Not so much is expected of me now. But I think I can play well and I have to prove it to myself. I was telling [Rod] Laver today, I still get nervous about my performance. I don't want to go out there and play like a dog. I think I played well today, though—as well as anyone on the court. I have better control over myself now than I did in the early sixties. I have a different attitude because I have a confidence that I'm doing what I should be doing. Of course, I don't have *everything* under control now, but I've won more matches lately.

"I had been putting feelings first and faith last, and I have to reverse that. It's not important, really, whether I *feel* good or bad. I feel better today after having won, but I'm learning to put faith first, even when I don't have that good a feeling. Faith helps me get over my depressions when I lose, though it doesn't eliminate them entirely."

Recalling that some top athletes claim they try to develop a "killer instinct," a tremendously fierce competitive urge to win, I asked Dennis if he had experienced attitudes like that.

"I used to feel that way before I became involved in the Christian thing," he said. "But I don't feel the same now. I want to win and do my best, but it's not the end of the world if I don't. I don't want to 'kill' or humiliate an opponent. In the long run, it would hurt me as much as him. Also, I don't play

60

deliberately to distract an opponent. Some guys do it and get away with it, but in the long run it hurts them. I do the best I can, compete hard, fight to win. If I have an opening to hit a ball at a guy, I'll do it."

"Suppose you're way ahead of a guy," I asked. "Would you let up on your game because you feel sorry for him?"

"Probably not," Dennis said. "You're never sure you'll win a match—you might trip and break an ankle. I try to end the match as quickly as possible. Professional tennis is a business, and the main object is to win. There are a lot of verses in the Bible to support this idea: 'Whatever your task, work heartily, as serving the Lord and not men . . .' (Col 3:23). Also, in I Corinthians 9:24: 'Do you not know that in a race all the runners compete, but only one receives the prize? So run that you may obtain it.' "

Thinking about how embarrassing it might be for me to play someone of Ralston's caliber, I asked, "Suppose you and I were hitting a few balls around, or maybe playing a few games for fun. Do you mean you'd knock me off the court?"

He grinned and shook his head. "Not if I'm playing for fun. That's different."

"Suppose you were playing in a tournament and your opponent has just hit a shot that a linesman wrongfully called 'out,' " I continued, wanting to explore a little further the possible tension between his faith and his work. "Would you give the point to your opponent?"

He became serious and pondered the question for a moment. "I've given a lot of thought to that. If it's out and the linesman makes a wrong call, I'll do anything I can to change the call. Certain players won't, though. [Pancho] Gonzales says you should go by the linesman's calls. He had the killer instinct for sure."

I grimaced and said, "I was a ballboy once for Gonzales when he came through Dallas as a touring pro. I threw a ball to the wrong place during his match and he took me to task. He was really sarcastic and humiliated me in front of five thousand spectators."

"He can be very gentle and nice and warm too," Dennis said. Dennis often seemed to want to get along well with people and emphasized the good qualities rather than the bad. But I wondered about his attitude toward tennis star Jimmy Connors, who had reportedly refused to play Davis Cup because Ralston was the captain. Connors' opposition to Ralston was generally regarded as a key factor in his dismissal from the Cup leadership. By chance, Ralston was scheduled to play Connors in the first round of singles in the U. S. Pro indoor tournament, and I asked whether this might turn into a grudge match.

"I have no personal problems with Jimmy," Dennis said. "Most of the problems started with [Bill] Riordan [Connors' former manager]. Actually, I never had any personal outbreaks with Riordan, either—all the arguments were in the press. Riordan didn't like Donald Dell, my agent, because he felt the Davis Cup was actually run by Dell. [The problem started when Jimmy] offered to play in the Davis Cup final in 1973, though he wasn't available to play the other matches. I said I appreciated his offer to play, but I felt it was like Wilt Chamberlain sitting out the entire basketball season and then saying, 'I want to play in the playoffs.' It's a matter of fairness. I appreciated the offer, but I couldn't accept. I think it's interesting I'm playing Connors here, though. I am nervous about the match, and I hope I play well. I think I will."

"How are your relations with Connors now?" I asked.

"Quite amicable," he said. "I've been around him more in the locker rooms and at tournaments. As a matter of fact, I'm playing doubles with him next week at an independent tournament in Boca Raton, Florida."

"Really?" I exclaimed, somewhat surprised.

"Yes," Dennis continued. "We get along, and he's a very good doubles player. I think he's gotten tired of the image he had. He likes to be liked, the same as anybody else. I know Connors will be trying hard, and so will I. And our decision to play together was not for the press. It wasn't symbolic. I'm doing this because he's a good doubles player."

"It's also a smart move," I said, public relations always on my mind.

"I didn't do it for that reason," Dennis emphasized. "I laughingly thought about it [the press impact] before I asked him to play. But I like to win tournaments. I'm in the business to win. So I approached him. I asked him to play and he said, 'Sure, I'd love to.'"

This willingness to take the initative as peacemaker with old adversaries was a far cry from the pre-Christian "bad boy of tennis" that I had read about in the sixties. I also found that Ralston's faith had given him a sense of perspective and purpose about what many people would have regarded as the final blow to a career—his dismissal from the Davis Cup. But I learned he had quickly perceived his firing as God's will.

"I'm kind of glad I got out of the Davis Cup," he said. "I began to think only I could do the job. It was my thing, and that was the wrong attitude."

"Do you think maybe you had turned the Davis Cup into a kind of idol?"

"Yeah, exactly," he replied. "Linda and I definitely talked about that and decided we felt that way. As it happened, losing the job made me think more about my life. And I was also motivated to get back in shape and think about playing again. It took me three months, getting up at seven every morning. But I think God made all this possible. And the extra time gave me an opportunity to work with young kids who want to go on the pro tour. That's what I do best—coaching. I think God is moving me in that direction because I believe I've had a good influence on a lot of young kids."

His skill at coaching became apparent to me when I mentioned I'd been having some trouble with my own serve.

"Let's see your service motion," he said authoritatively as he shoved one of his rackets at me.

I swung the racket several times at an imaginary ball, and he immediately noticed that I was twisting my body around too much on the follow-through. Sure enough, when I got on a court the following weekend, I could see an immediate improvement. As far as I'm concerned, any tennis pro who can diagnose a problem that fast in a hotel room has to have a great future in teaching and coaching. His designation as player-coach of the Los Angeles Strings of World Team Tennis apparently shows somebody else agrees with me.

A few days after our discussion, Dennis managed to achieve several other immediate goals that prompted a New York *Times* sports writer to credit him as "the frontrunner for the comeback man of the year in tennis." Although he lost to Jimmy Connors in his singles match, he and Rod Laver went on to score a series of devastating upsets and win the Pro In-door Doubles Championship. Then he was designated playing captain of the United States World Cup team, which participates in annual matches against the top Australian tennis players. He led his players—including Jimmy Connors—to a lopsided 6–1 upset over the Australians, who had won the cup for several previous years. Dennis teamed with Arthur Ashe to win the final doubles match.

The future for Dennis Ralston will undoubtedly include other such successes. But regardless of what he achieves on the tennis court, there's a sense of divine perspective in his life now which potentially gives every endeavor a deeper meaning, a purpose and direction that he never had before. Since his comeback is with Christ, he really can't lose.

# Chapter 5

# *Reunion with a Boyhood Buddy*

## DAVID NELSON

When I first saw David Nelson—the oldest son of the old "The Adventures of Ozzie and Harriet" television show—as he walked into the hotel lobby in Hollywood, I half-expected him to recognize me. He was wearing a baggy old sports coat and sweater, and, except for a few extra lines on his face, looked exactly as he had on the screen. We had only conversed on the telephone, but I somehow felt we were good friends who had just been out of touch for a while. He and his brother, Ricky, had "grown up" with me and my brother and sister during the 1950s and '60s. Their televison family had, in a sense, been an extension of my real family. I had watched him wrestle with school and personal problems, joke with friends, and hassle his parents the same way I did. I really believed I *knew* David, and I thought that in some way he must know me too.

When I walked over and introduced myself, I discovered immediately that the TV image and the real person were one and the same. He was the self-effacing, modest, shy, all-American boy I had seen for a dozen years or more. Although I had told him I would meet him wherever he wanted, he had insisted on coming over to the Continental Hyatt House where I was staying. He obviously wanted to avoid inconveniencing me.

We settled down at a table near the balcony in my room, with the palm trees of Sunset Boulevard blowing gently in the breeze outside the window and the smoggy Los Angeles skyline in the background. David seemed a little nervous, and was anxious to please and solicitious. But despite his slight uneasiness, it was obvious to me that he had a message he wanted to share. After a few minutes of casual conversation, in which I identified myself as a fellow Christian, we were talking like old boyhood chums who are eagerly picking up the loose ends of a deep but temporarily interrupted relationship. The first thing I wanted to know was the exact way he had come to accept Christ.

"I had a lot of friends who were Christians," he said. "I myself was baptized as an Episopalian and had a formal Christian education in a Methodist church, though I stopped going to services when I was eighteen. My folks never took me to church, never attended as far as I know. I considered myself to be a Christian because I wasn't a Jew."

It struck me as ironic—and I told him so—that a wholesome family like the Nelsons would not be a Christian family.

"Yeah. Everybody who watched the 'Ozzie and Harriet' show had assumed our family was a churchgoing family, but we weren't," he said. "In fact, the first person who told me I *wasn't* a Christian really shocked me. It was as though he was telling me I wasn't a nice guy."

"Who told you that?" I asked. It's often struck me that such bold witnessing is all too rare, because few Christians, it seems, are willing to risk possible rejection by confronting people with a clear, decisive presentation of Jesus' message of salvation.

"It was a friend of mine who's a trapeze artist," he said. "I got interested in trapeze work during the mid-sixties when I played a trapeze 'catcher' in the movie *The Big Circus,* with Victor Mature and Gilbert Roland. I started working out with people who did stunt work and then joined a touring trapeze act that played with various circuses in the United States, Germany, and the Philippines.

"I was usually an extra, added attraction—you know, 'David

66

Nelson is the guest artist'—that sort of thing. My first trapeze instructor, Bob Yerkes, a stunt man, was the first to mention Christ to me. I performed in his trapeze team during the summer months—we both worked as catchers. I didn't care about his witnessing at first. I believed in the Ten Commandments and tried to live a good life. I felt my image was good and I wasn't looking for anything. It was sometimes a drag with Bob because he'd get me up at five-thirty in the morning to go to Christian businessmen's breakfasts. I'd say, 'Gee, Bob, it's not enough that we do three shows a day. But now you get me up this early! I usually don't even get up to eat breakfast!' But I liked him and felt if he was this eager to get Christ into my life, the least I could do was go with him."

Although Bob's persistence got on his nerves, David found himself beginning to question the meaning of his life. Then his wife convinced him to start going to church because she wanted their children to have some exposure to Christianity. David found he actually enjoyed the experience.

"But then Bob told me just attending church regularly didn't make me a Christian," David said. "He was such a frank, honest person. I'd never heard that before. I believe many people who go to church don't believe in Christ. They may believe in God, but they haven't made a commitment to Christ."

David refused to make a complete commitment to Christ at this point, though, because of an intellectual block. "I didn't believe Jesus Christ and God were one," he recalled. "My basic battle was to understand how there could be one person in three. As I listened to sermons in the Lutheran church we were attending, I had a constant inner fight to understand the principle of the Trinity. Emotionally, I wanted to accept it, but intellectually I couldn't."

Then in 1972 David reached a critical point in his life. The reruns on the "Ozzie and Harriet" show would be coming to an end soon, and he needed to settle on another career. He had had some experience directing television programs, and he decided this was the field he liked best. So without any help from his Nelson family connections, he landed his first job with an outside company as a director of a dealership film for Volkswagen. His assignment involved some on-location work in West Germany.

"We were setting up to shoot some things from the top of a church in Bavaria," he recalled. "The crew had to go get the keys to the church loft, and I was left there sitting by myself in the church. As I stared at the altar, I wondered what my family was doing back in the States, and I realized, since it was Sunday morning there, that they were all in church. Then I began to ponder how I could accept the Trinity in my heart. I knew I could lie to everybody and say I'd accepted the idea, but I really couldn't do that honestly.

"It was a dark day, and the church was very dim inside because there weren't many windows. It was a huge, cavernous Gothic sanctuary, and I felt very small. As I looked at the altar, I thought how beautiful it was. And I thought how much more beautiful everything might be if I could accept Christ by faith, without trying to understand every theological problem. 'How can I accept God as three in one?' I wondered. Then an answer entered my mind: 'Maybe acceptance is the first step. Accept by faith, and the answer will come to you.' As I thought that, a cloud opened up outside. The sun came out, and a beam of light streamed through a stained-glass window and hit the altar. Suddenly the gold on the altar was illuminated. I said, 'Okay, that's enough for me!' There was a physical feeling, an exhilaration inside me, and I just started to laugh."

There was no one around that David felt he could share the experience with, so he kept it to himself, mulled over it. "But I definitely changed as a human being after that," he said. "It's hard to explain to someone because they could say, 'Oh, yeah, that's a wonderful coincidence.' But that happened to me when I needed the most help in my life. I was there and ready to accept. It was so startling. The answer to my question was that the first step of any belief or philosophy is faith. Then as you get involved, you understand things you couldn't understand before. You don't study and learn and resolve all the questions and then come by logic to the belief that Jesus was God on earth. You *can't first* figure that out, and *then* get faith. It's just the reverse. You must accept by faith, and then the other answers flow logically.

"After I accepted Christ, the intellectual answers to the Trinity problem became clearer. I realized, for example, that many things, not just God, can be three in one. Water can be liquid, steam, or ice. A woman can be a daughter, mother, and sister at the same time. There are plenty of answers about religion for intellectuals, but I don't think you can prove faith. And I don't think God wants you to prove it. He wants you to accept it. How do you prove your father is really your father? I think you get more from your real father by just accepting his parenthood, rather than by questioning it. It's the same with your heavenly Father."

His conversion didn't immediately introduce David Nelson into a happy, carefree existence, however. Even as he sat across the table from me in that hotel room, he was still recovering from a traumatic personal tragedy which had almost devastated him when he returned from that Volkswagen job in Germany. "Just after I accepted Christ as my Savior, my marriage fell apart," he told me, explaining that his wife had been attracted to someone else. "I found out about my marriage as soon as I landed in California. I came back to that situation and I thought, 'How could this happen? Is this what happens to you when you accept God—someone drops a ton of bricks on you?' At first, I felt betrayed by God. But I started reading the Bible and attending study classes and prayer therapy groups."

One of the most helpful passages of Scripture that David found was Luke 11:24–26: "In those verses, Jesus talks about the demons you let out of yourself when you open the doors [of your life] to let the Lord come in. You clean your house of demons, but then it's a nice place to which the demons may return. You let one demon out, and seven want to come back, Jesus says. That's exactly what happened to me. I had cleaned my house and if there was a demon in me I had gotten rid of him. But apparently he brought seven of his friends back. I learned Christians are not immune to these attacks, and the important thing is not to leave a [spiritual] vacuum. You have to begin to grow spiritually. Satan hates to lose us, so we're constantly bombarded. We have to allow the Lord to fill the vacuum in our lives so Satan can't get back in."

As David tried to patch his marriage back together during the next two years, he threw himself, perhaps prematurely, into speaking for Christ at public rallies. "About a month after my conversion, my pastor, a Lutheran minister, asked if I would speak at a youth rally at our church," he said. "That put me on the spot because I was a very new Christian. I knew little about the Bible, and I knew they didn't want to hear me give a sermon. They wanted to hear my personal testimony, how I accepted Christ. I couldn't tell you today what I said—I think I was operating on adrenalin. The voice on tape didn't even sound like my real voice.

"Then I spoke at Anaheim, in front of ten thousand Lutheran Sunday School teachers. There were some very heavy people on the dais, and I have no idea what I said. Still, I think it was effective because people had smiles on their faces afterwards."

"I wonder if you were facing what a lot of famous new Christians face—too much exposure too soon?" I remarked. "Do you think you were being exploited by church people?"

He thought for a moment and replied, "I didn't feel it then, but I started to feel leery when smaller groups interested in fund-raising began to approach me. I felt limited in being a voice for Christ since I knew so little about the Bible. A lot of people asked me to speak during that period—I guess I was a name, or people were familiar with me. And it does seem people just like to hear new Christians. But it's tough. Someone from Billy Graham's organization told me I shouldn't say yes to everything." David took this advice and turned his attention more to Bible study and his marital problems, which had been getting worse.

"I couldn't find a way to rectify the whole [marriage] situation as far as Christ was concerned," he explained. "All I could think of was that God says when you marry someone, it should be for life. It's a permanent bond, with God as your witness. I just didn't believe in divorce. I ended up talking to a couple of pastors, and I told them I had searched the Bible over but saw no place where the Lord wants you to stay with evil. There were two conflicting things: staying married no matter what, and stepping away from evil. After long conversations, people who knew the Bible better than I did agreed: it had never worked out, so the only way was for me to get out. My family [Ozzie, Harriet, and Ricky] were intelligent enough to realize separation was the best answer, but it was tough. My dad was sick with cancer and had just recently written a book about the entire family. I hesitated to fight with all the weapons I had."

70

But divorce proceedings were started, and the divorce became final just a few months before David and I talked in Hollywood. He was in a state of transition in many ways when I saw him, and though he appeared confident about his abilities as a director, he seemed somewhat apprehensive about his prospects. For one thing, he was thirty-nine years old and still trying to put together his new career as an independent director. His work as a trapeze artist had ended several years before, when he realized there was no future in it: "I quit the trapeze act after I performed on a television special on the 'Hollywood Palace' program," he recalled. "We caught a three and a half [somersault] for the first time on nationwide TV. People had been catching it for a while, but never before a major network audience. The only publicity we got was a little squib in *TV Guide,* which said this was the first time for a three and a half. I thought. 'Gee, for the hours I've put in over the last five years, if that's all it gets, I could walk down Sunset Boulevard and hit somebody and get more coverage than that.' So that was the last time I performed."

Another reason he was concerned about his job outlook was that he needed the extra income. "Before I was twenty-one, all my earnings from the TV series went into two trust funds," he explained. "One of the funds came due when I was twenty-one, and the other when I was thirty. Unfortunately, though the money was invested well, it was dispersed through my divorce. It's very important for me to work now."

It was hard for a person like myself, who grew up in relative obscurity in an ordinary middle-class home, to understand how wrenching the mid-life career crisis must be for a former child star like David Nelson. In a way he was like an old boyhood friend, but I also knew he had been much more than that. I wanted to find out more about how those early experiences as a member of everybody's favorite TV family had shaped the quiet, shy guy I was now talking to in this Hollywood hotel.

"You and Rick both had an all-American boy image—you were examples to a lot of us," I said. "Did you find that image hard to live up to in the *real* Nelson family situation?"

"Things about it were destructive," he admitted. "Instead of growing up naturally, we probably tried to fulfill the image of the TV role. We were the only real family on TV and we used

71

our own names. It was like baring your chest in front of millions of people. You can't reveal yourself totally on TV—it would be too uninteresting—but we did insert a great deal of ourselves in our roles. I say 'role' in quotes, because I had to believe David Nelson was really the character I played. It became a sort of Jekyll and Hyde situation, because there were times when you weren't sure [who you were] at home. The TV studio was like our home, complete with a refrigerator—we'd actually eat there on the set. I spent the majority of fifteen years of my life on that set. My father was the director-producer. My mother was always there. The family was constantly together.

"But on the whole, I think the typecast of the All-American boy was no problem for me. It was easy for David Nelson to be the same David on the set. I didn't start smoking until I was out of college; I got in bed fairly early; I participated in sports."

"But what about kids you knew on the outside—didn't they look at you as different from other boys?" I wondered.

"I was lucky with that," he replied. "The kids I went to school with didn't consider me anything but David. Most of [the star-struck attitude] came from people from Omaha who came to California for the summer. A friend of mine would come over and say, 'I can't understand it. Joyce from Omaha wants to see you. She's dying; she'll have a heart attack unless she sees you.' I could understand, but to him I was just David. It wasn't until I got to college, at the University of Southern California, that people started turning around to look at me, and I started to feel self-conscious. But one day I was walking down a campus sidewalk and a student carrying some books was coming from the other direction. He had been in the Korean War and had lived through some disastrous fires. He'd been terribly burned. I used to think, 'How can I study with people looking at me? Poor me!' But now I thought, 'If a guy like this can hack it, I have no problems at all.' That straightened me out a lot, because my problems couldn't touch this guy's."

This sensitivity and sense of perspective on his own situation has apparently stayed with David as part of his Christian experience. When the "Ozzie and Harriet" show stopped production, it seemed he was being put into "forced retirement," he said. But he doesn't plan to be one of those Christians who waits around passively for some special divine revelation about his future. "I think seeking God's will for your life [in the wrong way] can be the greatest Christian hangup," he said. "It's a big cop-out to say you're finding God's will by just sitting, waiting forever. It's up to us to use what He's given us. He gave us a lot, and He expects us to use the tools He's given us."

Although he's strongly self-reliant, David does believe that prayer is an integral part in finding God's will for his career life. "You have to talk to God," he declared. "A lot of actors will mention timing and luck, but I think God has a lot of control over those things. I believe that after you've used all your own efforts and do everything you can do for yourself, God's will becomes evident. God gave us all He could when He put us here, and we have to release our talents to the Lord."

As we discussed his job possibilities, I learned his immediate plans were to continue trying to get jobs directing industrial films. But he also has a deep-rooted desire to direct Christian films including those which churches and denominations could use for educational purposes.

"I've had a lot of hesitancy about pursuing this, though, because some people might think I'm talking advantage," he said. "They might say I'm using the fact that I'm a Christian to get a job."

"We've discussed the same issue at a small weekly prayer group that I attend back in New York," I said. "Some of the fellows think it's a good thing to do business with other Christians, but others feel as you do—that it's better to avoid all appearance of profiting from your faith."

He indicated he still hadn't resolved the issue himself. But he said, "I know I'd like to do Christian films. For example, you might produce a film cassette showing how a Christian couple deals with a family problem."

"Sounds almost like a Christian 'Ozzie and Harriet,'" I responded, smiling. "Or maybe a Christian soap opera."

"Yes, even though I'm in commercial and industrial sales filming right now, I'd really rather go into a Christian area with this," he said, almost seeming to make up his mind more definitely as we talked.

"You mean you'd like to sell spiritual concepts through film, rather than automobiles or something?" I asked.

"Right—selling the Lord," he agreed.

When David Nelson finally got up to say good-bye, I realized I was feeling quite close to him as a result of our "reunion." I knew he still faced the same questions and confusions he had brought to our discussion. And as I watched him walk across Sunset Boulevard, I found myself desperately wanting him to find the precise niche that God has for him. After all, he was even more than my spiritual brother—he had been practically a member of my own family for a dozen years.

Chapter 6

# *The Boone Factor*
## PAT BOONE

After David Nelson's conversion, as he was trying to solidify his new faith, he stopped briefly at a spiritual watering hole that many Los Angeles Christians have used—the prayer and sharing meetings at Pat and Shirley Boone's home in Beverly Hills. A majority of the performers I talked to not only knew Pat, they also considered him to be a "good friend." Many had been influenced spiritually by him to one degree or another.

Nelson's path of Christian progress has veered away from Boone's tongues-speaking, Charismatic Renewal Movement approach. But for a time, he found Christian fellowship there, just as Robert Goulet and Carol Lawrence got advice from Pat about churches they might attend. Though Pat would never admit it, I became convinced during my travels that the Boones' house is a major spiritual focal point—just as were the homes of Priscilla and Aquila in Corinth, or Lydia in Macedonia during New Testament times (Acts 16,18).

Pat Boone reached the peak of his popularity as a singer when I was in high school during the 1950s. The image I had of him before our discussion was the usual, frivolous one of a guy with white buck shoes and a gushy, goody-goody, gee-whiz personality. I couldn't have been more mistaken. During our entire talk he was totally serious, and every other point he made was supported by Biblical authority and presented with persuasive, coherent logic. Was this really the same guy who had crooned "Love Letters in the Sand" and vaulted into old jalopies with Terry Moore in the less than memorable 1957 movie *Bernardine?*

In those early days and especially in the decade that followed, "I wasn't letting God, my Father, call the shots in my life," Pat told me. "I wanted to run things myself. Like the prodigal son [Luke 15], I gradually took my inheritance and ran off with it. I got off into that far country and, in many ways, like the prodigal son, I was eating pig food."

Pat emphasized that he had been converted—initially accepted Christ as his Savior—when he was thirteen years old and had been baptized in water. Even though he gradually drifted away from an obedient relationship with God in the years that followed, he still considers himself to have been a Christian in those days. He was just not a very effective one.

His faith had been tested by reading secular arguments against Christianity. "There were times in my traveling when I read cynical books, like Mark Twain's *Letters from the Earth,* in which he ridicules a naïve faith in the Bible. He emphasizes apparent contradictions in the Scriptures and seemingly merciless acts that God did, such as wiping out thousands of people [in the Old Testament]. That kind of stuff will shake your faith."

The further he drifted away from God's guidance, "the more loused up my life got," Pat said. "I was having marital and family difficulties, career and financial problems. But I could still hear the Father calling me to come home.

"You know, Bill," he told me, "even when I was away in that 'far country,' there were times—and I've often thought gratefully about them—when I used to stand outside at night in front of our house here, with Shirley and the girls asleep. I'd walk around outside and look at the stars. I felt much closer to the Lord at night than at any other time. I'd look up at the sky, and there was no way I could deny the existence of God."

He believes that the Holy Spirit began to use friends like Clint Davidson, David Wilkerson, and George Otis to draw him back to the faith. "There was an active agency of the Holy Spirit at work in those people and in my own heart," Pat explained. "Jesus said, in John 6, that no man can come to the Father except the Father draw him. So I gradually began to feel, because of a convergence of things, that it was God calling me and wooing me by the Spirit. I perceived it was the Spirit of God, but I had not surrendered myself at that point. I was still trying to chart my own course, despite God's constant wooing.

"I sometimes use the example of a compass. Above the equator, that needle will point to the North Pole. You can't see the North Pole, but it's there. Every compass needle in the world points toward it, and that's evidence of it. There's also something in the heart of every man—unless he's totally dead spiritually—that points that way, that is evidence of the existence of God."

In talking with Pat, his three friends—Otis, Wilkerson, and Davidson—emphasized spiritual renewal and submission to God in terms of the Charismatic, or neo-Pentecostal, movement. They said it was important to have a "baptism of the Spirit," which would lead to gifts of the Spirit, like tongues, healing, and prophecy [see 1 Corinthians 12]. Although Pat's wife, Shirley, experienced this baptism of the Spirit, Pat found himself facing an intellectual block. "I had doubts about my own ability and commitment," he said. "I've always been a rational person. I've operated rationally since I was twelve or thirteen. I wanted to know there was a 'Thus saith the Lord' for everything I did. I was afraid to surrender myself to an emotional experience. Deep inside me was a need to know I was on solid ground because I knew if I experienced something only on an emotional level, I might be out on a limb that could be sawed off."

"In your book *A New Song,* it struck me that in seeking the 'baptism of the Spirit' you were looking for the gift rather than the Giver," I noted. "You didn't really fight God openly at this point, did you? It seemed to me you were almost ignorant you were putting yourself first."

"Yes," he agreed. "There were times I'd prostrate myself in a hotel room and say, 'Okay, Lord, do it to me! I'm ready!' But I'd be disappointed because nothing happened. I was actually looking for an experience to create faith. But Jesus said the signs and wonders *follow* to confirm faith, rather than create it. Some people just surrender to Him and something delightful happens to them almost immediately. But I guess the Lord knew I needed to know I was on solid ground Scripturally.

While I was praying for something to happen to me, I was looking into the Bible at the same time, talking to other Christians, and trying to find God's validation of this."

But then Pat—much as David Nelson had done—began to realize that his trust in God would have to transcend these intellectual objections. An effective faith was something which could come only from outside the narrow limits of his own intellect. "Paul said in the first chapter of 1 Corinthians that God has deliberately chosen the foolish things of this world to confound the wise," Pat said, relying as he always does on Scriptural authority. "It's the trademark of the Lord to do things in a way that doesn't appeal to our logic, our intellect, our reasoning power. He won't allow anyone to come to Him on terms of man's own understanding. We must come on faith, which involves accepting things we can't understand or comprehend. I had to do it this way, even though it works against every part of me. But God said do it, so I did it. Then the understanding comes later."

Pat applied this insight to what he knew of his wife's commitment and obedience to the Holy Spirit, and suddenly things began to make more sense. "Shirley didn't go into the Scriptures," he said. "She just asked for the baptism of the Holy Spirit, as George Otis told her to do. It didn't take a lot of Bible study for her to do this. Yet the Bible says the Father will give the Holy Spirit to those who ask. Then I realized how Shirley and her childlike, trusting faith had come to the Lord. She had offered herself in *every* way, even vocally. At first, she did speak some words which she knew didn't mean anything. But after her voluntary surrender, she was met by the Lord and, forty-five minutes later, she spoke in a prayer language she had never learned."

As for himself, Pat realized, "I still had one foot in the boat. I was unwilling to commit myself totally for fear I'd have a synthetic experience that I'd later regret. Intellectually, I wanted to hang on to something familiar, even if it wasn't secure. I wanted God to sweep me off my feet with something I couldn't deny."

In a decisive meeting with George Otis, Pat's "baptism of the Spirit" finally occurred, and caused him to sing in a strange, guttural prayer language.

78

"Did you get emotional at the time?" I asked. "Was there any physical feeling that gripped you?"

Pat replied that, unlike many such Pentecostal experiences, "there was no sense of emotion when it happened. It was just a surrender and a stepping out by faith. I spoke some words softly but didn't feel anything. The 'baptism of the Holy Spirit' is not primarily a matter of what you feel. For me, it was purely and simply the same kind of thing that happened when I was baptized in water. It was a matter of a decision, and I knew it was right. After my water baptism as a boy, there was a glow and a sense of well-being and cleanness. Later, as I looked back on that moment, I realized that I'd done what God had wanted, that I was a child of God and had started my life over again, clean and fresh. My sense of being in the family of God grew after that.

"After the 'baptism of the Spirit,' I began to sing [in tongues], but the goosebumps or the feeling of a new dimension in God and the Spirit didn't come until afterwards, as I was still singing this song. There was this curious Hebraic turn in the words and melody. It was almost as though I was standing back, listening to these words. It was not my doing, but I was just hearing it. I knew something was happening, but I was detached. Then the goosebumps came, and the rise of emotion, as I began to believe and sense this thing that was happening to me. But God was not meeting me primarily on a feeling or intellectual level, but on a deeper spiritual level. When the goosebumps and emotion finally came, the feeling wasn't overwhelming, but just a response to what I realized had happened and was happening. A lot of folks think that the 'baptism of the Holy Spirit' is a sudden rush of emotion, and especially that glossolalia, or tongues, is an overwhelming emotional experience. To some people it may be, but for me it wasn't."

"Do you think God chose a song for you because you're a singer?" I asked.

"I think so," he said. "He seems to tailor-make experiences for people—like fingerprints and other aspects of our personalities and bodies. I think this was His way of dealing with me. I've talked to other people who have had other kinds of experiences. Some even laugh in their prayer language."

As he talked, I realized that Pat Boone and I are a lot alike.

In the past I've sometimes been accused of being aloof, reserved, unemotional, and overly rational, especially by casual acquaintances. But then I myself had a particularly intense encounter with the Holy Spirit, and my emotions seemed to relax, to become freer than ever before. Although I used to steel myself against shedding a tear after a powerful film, book, or Christian testimony, now I often let them flow. Wondering if Pat was undergoing the same transformation, I said, "You mentioned you're not an emotional person?"

"That's right. I'm a very controlled person. I have one of those invisible sprinkler systems, almost like a battle station which sounds an alarm so I can squelch the tears. I don't do that so much now. I find that things take me more by surprise, and I date this back to my 'baptism of the Spirit' experience."

"I've had almost the same thing happen to me," I said. "I was a much more rationally oriented person myself until I had an experience with the Holy Spirit about a year ago that was similar to yours."

"Yeah?" Pat said, apparently interested in what I was saying.

"When riding on a train, I was overcome with thankfulness at how good God had been to me," I explained. "Almost involuntarily, I began to cry and felt compelled to praise God in strange, fluent sounds. An overwhelming sense of His love gripped me. I could hardly control my exuberance when I got off the train at Penn Station in Manhattan. Instead of the usual wariness and defensiveness I feel on New York City streets, I felt a great love for everyone I saw because I knew God loved them too. It was almost as though His love was channeled through me to them. A powerful force—the Holy Spirit— seemed to fill me and carry me along the sidewalk. The physical sensation subsided after about a half hour, but the sense of love and inner joy stayed with me for several hours. And I've found my emotions have loosened up considerably since this experience."

"Isn't it a great thing?" Pat exclaimed.

"I think it is," I said.

"I was a prisoner of my mind," he sighed, pondering the struggle he had gone through with God. "I tried to control my feelings, but I envied people like my wife who had more spontaneous responses. I just didn't seem to [have that spontaneity]. I think I was afraid of being embarrassed, so I held [my emotions] back. It was an automatic thing with me. Now, I don't cry so much at sad things, as at happy things. When people tell me about how great God has been to them, about some spiritual breakthrough, that brings emotions and tears to my eyes quicker than any sad thing. When I hear of something sad, my response is: 'Let's do something—let's pray about it.' I know God doesn't want to be defeated and wants to bring us through that experience. But I'm more easily moved to tears now, and I'm glad of it."

One of the reasons that the Boones have become such a focal point for Christianity in Hollywood is that Pat not only helps people find a deep relationship with Christ; he also baptizes those who don't want to go to conventional pastors and churches. "I've baptized over three hundred in our swimming pool," he said. "A lot of folks meet the Lord in prayer groups or in other meetings not affiliated with any church. They don't know what church they want to be in. Sometimes when the weather is good, ministers who teach in these house groups have brought over from ten to thirty people to be baptized on a Saturday morning. It's a convenient time, and we did that most Saturday mornings for a year. I'd sit in the water and baptize folks, and then encourage them to continue in their house Bible study, but also to join some organized church.

"I've cut way down on this lately because I've seen more and more churches begin to preach the full Gospel, the new life. And I equate baptism with a wedding ceremony. A baptism in a pool or river is good, but it's sort of like having an elopement to start a marriage. I believe a church wedding has an advantage because we need to establish fellowship with other believers on a regular basis in a church. I've found a lot of times folks would be baptized here but would never get into a church fellowship. I've seen them wane in enthusiasm.

"But I'm willing to baptize people if I really feel like the Lord wants me to. Sometimes when I've told people to go to their own ministers, the minister has refused to baptize them because either his church doesn't teach much about baptism or the minister says, 'You were baptized as a child and I won't baptize you again.' In other words, he had hangups about it himself. If the person begins to get desperate about it because

81

his own minister won't baptize him, I'll do it if I'm satisfied myself that this is what the Lord wants."

"Have you found many people come to you just because they want to be baptized by Pat Boone?" I asked.

"That's always a possibility," he said seriously. "You know, in the first century the works of Paul loomed with great weight, and he thanked God that he had baptized [only a handful of Christians] in Corinth (I Corinthians 1:14–16). He could see the church was dividing up along personalities. And I could see some folks wanted to come here because they had heard about the baptisms at Pat Boone's house, and they wanted to say, 'Yes, I was baptized there too.'"

I laughed and almost said, "In other words, you were afraid of creating a group of 'Boonies' rather than Christians"—but I thought better of it. Pat was such a serious guy that I was afraid he might misunderstand, or even think I was trying to make fun of his religious experience.

"I always encourage people to be baptized in their home churches now," he continued. "Spirit-filled churches like the one where I'm an elder—the Church on the Way in Van Nuys."

"By the way," I said, "Robert Goulet told me a few days ago that he was thinking about coming over there next Sunday."

"Oh, man, I hope so," Pat replied, apparently genuinely concerned about Bob and his wife, Carol Lawrence. This conversation took place just before the two famous singers got involved in separation proceedings. "I've invited them again. Bob raised his hand and made a recommitment at the Church on the Way, and Carol has made her commitment or recommitment —I don't know how she describes it—at Bel Air Presbyterian."

Such comments impressed me again with how involved Pat Boone is in the spiritual growth of many famous Christians. Remembering that David Nelson had told me the Christian community had pushed him too quickly into a position of leadership, I asked Boone, "Have you ever felt exploited or pressured to appear before Christian groups because you're a celebrity?"

"I resist that and try to look at any situation to see if there's anybody else better qualified," Pat said. "Some celebrities have no background in the Scriptures, and then they're put in front of a crowd to speak when they're not ready. That's happened a lot. Though it hasn't been true of me, I've seen it happen. I know of a couple of big entertainers who have made commitments to the Lord in our home or soon after a Bible study here. The word spreads like wildfire, and people besiege them. An older Christian may walk up to these new Christians in restaurants and say, 'Oh, praise the Lord! I understand you've given your heart to Jesus!' And the person cringes because he or she may be with people who don't understand the whole thing.

"Jonathan Winters told me he took his fourteen-year-old daughter to a worship service. She had asked him to take her to church, and he thought it was a good idea. He enjoyed the service, the old associations, the old yearnings. He was really glad he'd come until afterwards when people bombarded him for autographs. And the minister said, 'It's great to have you! We need people like you, and we're having a benefit in about two weeks.' But Johnny stopped him and said, 'Listen, I don't have anything to give anybody. I'm here because I *need* something.' And he hasn't been back.

"Humanly, we get so excited about the conversion of a celebrity—an entertainer or a politician—as though he or she meant more than just somebody in a more ordinary walk of life. We push and pull them too fast, and it can really work against them."

"You've seen quite a few people accept Christ," I remarked. "I'm wondering if you see any common factors that might lead to a conversion or renewal experience?"

"Everybody's experience is unique," he replied. "But in the broadest terms, when we start to hear about entertainers or others who have serious problems, some of us actually feel a twinge of excitement and say, 'Praise the Lord!'—because most people have to come to an end of themselves and their own resources. It all goes back to the prodigal son. Before we can start to consider how much we do need God, we vacillate and try to find alternatives. Our relationship with Him must be the most important thing in the world, and we're all afraid of such a commitment."

"What advice would you give to a person who wants to find Christ?" I asked.

"I wouldn't say you should *ask* for trouble or problems," Pat said. "But I'd say get still before God—be serious enough to take a day or two for this stillness. I've often advised people to fast for a day if they're really interested [in finding God]. I tell them to do without food for a day and make every hunger pang a prayer. I've seen really dramatic answers to that kind of prayer. God is waiting to reveal Himself to us and be real to us. Usually, we're like drowning men who, by our striving, kicking, and thrashing, actually drive away the swimmer who has come to save us. Lifesaving usually requires that the person who wants his life saved must get still and allow the rescuer to do his thing. It's the same with God. We have to just flow with the Spirit and surrender ourselves, ask the Lord to be real to us. Jesus promised signs and wonders would follow, but He also said in John 14:21 that 'He who has my commandments and keeps them, he it is who loves me; and he who loves me will be loved by my Father, and I will love him and manifest myself to him.'

"God *will* reveal Himself if you make yourself quiet enough. So I do encourage people to fast for a day—no food at all, though maybe some water or fruit juice. For most people that's a new experience, and I think God honors such a diligent search."

Although I've never found fasting to be amenable to my spiritually undisciplined stomach, I found myself agreeing wholeheartedly with Pat Boone's emphasis on persistent supplication and obedience to Christ as the only sure method for finding God's will. In fact, my interview with Pat marked the completion of some special answers to prayer in my own life.

As I had embarked on the interviews for this book, I realized that the main problem I would face would be getting enough celebrities together in the same place to make a trip to see them worth while. I soon learned, however, that most celebrities don't like to commit themselves too far in advance. "Call me when you get out here, and we'll set something up," was the usual response. As a result, on my first trip to Hollywood, the only definite commitment I had was for a discussion with Robert Goulet. Several other celebrities would only say, "Maybe." So I found myself racked by anxiety the week before I left, worried about whether or not I would get to talk to any other Christian performers or be left with a huge airplane and hotel bill, and only one interview to show for it.

In the past, I had frequently lectured my wife, Pam, about the virtues of not worrying about things you couldn't possibly control. I was a great advocate of committing those things to God, releasing them to His care, "letting go" of my own inadequate grip on them and allowing Him to shoulder my problems and worries. But now I got some of my own good advice in return. "You're always telling me to trust God, Bill," Pam said. "Now you should practice what you preach. It's obvious in this case you can't do anything about these uncertain appointments in California until you get out there. Quit worrying and let God take charge!"

Easy words to say, as I well knew—but very difficult to put into practice, especially since I knew hundreds of dollars were hanging in the balance. I found that intellectually and, in some sense, spiritually, I could give this problem to God. But *emotionally,* I still was in the grip of a great deal of anxiety. The tight feelings in the pit of my stomach testified to that. Why didn't God remove this anxiety?

After I arrived in Los Angeles and checked into the Continental Hyatt House in Hollywood, I was still worried and uncertain, but I kept in close touch with God through prayer. Gradually I found myself becoming detached from the situation and was able to stand back and watch Him work. I really began to believe with my whole being that He was in charge of my trip, and suddenly things began to fall into place. I finally got through to David Nelson, and he readily agreed to an interview the next day. Robert Goulet was already lined up, and I also pinned down Pat Boone. I was confident now that God was in control, so it didn't particularly bother me when I learned Carol Lawrence would not be available until after my return flight was scheduled to depart. Earlier in the week that might well have panicked me because I knew the airlines were on strike and it was nearly impossible to change reservations to New York. But I wasn't worried at all. In fact, I made this entry in my daily journal: "I'm willing now to let God take charge. If necessary, I'll cancel my plane reservation and trust He will provide something for me on stand-by. I'm calm, and have absolutely no anxiety. It's exciting!"

Shortly afterward, Carol Lawrence called me herself. I told her my situation with the airplanes, and she insisted I come over to talk to her before my plane was scheduled to leave. As I returned home, I was flying higher than my 747 airliner. Being obedient to God—trusting Him in a simple, childlike way—had done more for my complex, fluctuating interview schedule than any amount of worry. Jesus' words in the Sermon on the Mount, Matthew 6:27, kept running through my mind: "And which of you by being anxious can add one cubit to his span of life?"

Chapter 7

# Bob and Carol and Bill and God

## ROBERT GOULET AND CAROL LAWRENCE

Even on a first visit to the home of new friends, certain tell-tale signs may lead you to suspect that deep tensions and scars run below the surface amenities. The conversation may seem pleasant and the smiles genuine, but an occasional frustrated comment here or a skeptical expression there sometimes signal that the very foundations of the marriage are crumbling.

Because of the unusual pressures and temptations that confront them, celebrities—even those who are Christians—seem more susceptible than most of us to the insidious epidemic of marital discord that is destroying so many families across the nation. But it was a particular blow to many of their Christian fans and friends when Carol Lawrence and Robert Goulet announced their separation. As far as I know, I was the last journalist to interview them at their Beverly Hills home, only two weeks before they parted ways on New Year's Day, 1976.

Despite the creeping smog that mars the green valleys and obscures the rich mansions, Beverly Hills has always held a peculiar fascination for me. When I was stationed in Southern California several years ago with the Marine Corps, my wife

87

Pam and I enjoyed taking periodic drives through the winding, residential roads, lined with palm trees and tropical flowers. One of our favorite pastimes on these trips was to peek through the fences and foliage that surrounded the homes of celebrities and speculate about the pleasures and problems of living in such a rarefied atmosphere.

Perhaps the most mysterious tourist attraction was the Goulets' hilltop home—a veritable castle for America's king and queen of song. If you follow one of the "star maps" that are available on Hollywood newsstands, you'll find you have to shift your car into second gear and move steadily upward, over one short, exclusive street after another to the very top level of the smog belt. Finally, you reach a private driveway at the end of Briarcrest Lane.

Pam and I, as mere sightseers, had to stop at the signs that warned "No Trespassing" and "Beware of the Dogs!" so we weren't even able to catch a glimpse of the Goulet-Lawrence mansion. But during the Christmas season of 1975, after Robert Goulet had agreed to talk with me about his religious faith, I boldly instructed my cab driver to go on up to the top. It was an intriguing prospect. Not only was I going to have an inside view of the way this famous couple lived, but also I was going to get a glimpse of their deepest beliefs and spiritual experiences.

Our car climbed the narrow driveway at an even steeper incline, past blooming poinsettia and hibiscus bushes, until we reached a huge iron gate. Through the black bars I could see part of their splendid home, which nestled in trees and gardens on the top of the peak. Off to my left was a panoramic view of the rest of Beverly Hills and an expansive sky above, clear blue and smog-free.

My driver buzzed an intercom outside the gate and notified someone inside of our arrival, and the huge gates swung back automatically. But instead of Robert Goulet, five gigantic barking, growling dogs greeted us. I was so preoccupied with planning how I was going to get safely past the animals—one of which I later learned was half wolf—that I almost failed to notice a tall man who was standing on the front steps. He was wearing old, casual clothes, and I figured this must be a yard man or perhaps a dog trainer. At any rate, his presence gave me courage, so I held my breath, opened the cab door, and walked slowly through the howling pack. Finally, when one dog stopped barking and began licking my hand clutching my tape recorder, I knew I was almost home free. Before I could wipe away the animal's saliva, the tall fellow, who somehow was beginning to look vaguely familiar, stepped down to greet me. He stuck out his hand and said, "Hi, I'm Bob Goulet!"

I immediately knew I'd have to throw out most of my preconceptions of what the famous singer would be like. His rough-hewn informality contrasted sharply with the elegant manner and dress he often displays on stage, and he seemed leaner, older, and more rugged-looking than the slick "prettyboy" image he sometimes projected to me on TV. His black hair, tousled as though he had just rolled out of bed, was streaked around the sideburns with gray. Tight, tie-dyed jeans and an open-necked, form-fitting shirt revealed a hard, well-conditioned body that reminded me more of a rangy cowhand than a nightclub singer and Broadway musical star.

We moved through an elegant, airy living room and settled down in his den, which he had decorated with myriads of toy frogs—a hobby he's developed to stress the importance of keeping frogs on the shelf and out of his throat. Bob first told me a couple of funny, personal stories. Then he became more serious and began to describe his childhood religious experiences in an efficient, logical narrative. "I was born a Catholic, and I was a devout one," he said. "I even thought I might become a priest. But every time I walked down the street and saw a pretty girl, I said, 'That's out!' because priests, of course, aren't allowed to get married. God said, 'No, we don't want you in the priesthood!' "

Although he immediately established himself as a compelling storyteller, Bob demonstrated at the outset of our talk that he's also an impatient, aggressive guy with a rather short attention span. He expects his life—including discussions with writers—to be well organized, so he wasn't too happy when I learned, ten minutes into the interview, that my tape recorder wasn't working. I always glance periodically at the cassette wheels to be sure they're moving. My stomach jumped up into my throat when I saw they had stopped.

89

Looking at me as I stared at the recorder, Bob asked sharply, "Is that thing working?"

"No, something seems wrong," I replied.

He groaned as I nervously fiddled with the buttons and connections to try to locate the problem. Then the machine began again, and I sat back with a sigh of relief. But a few seconds later, it stopped once more. At that point, Bob rushed out of the room, and I was afraid for a moment I might have lost him. But he returned shortly with his own recorder.

"Here, use this," he ordered, and I was in no mood to argue. With an annoyed edge to his voice, he cleared his throat and asked, "What were we talking about?"

"You said, that, uh, that, uh . . ." I began, but he broke in again.

"Was that thing broken from the beginning?" he asked, still fuming.

"Yeah, apparently . . ."

"You mean from the *very* beginning?"

"Well, the important stuff was in the last couple of minutes," I replied as calmly as possible. "If you could just summarize . . ."

"No, I can't," he said with a stern look that made my heart fall. But then he smiled to let me know he was joking, leaned back in his chair, and began to go over what we had lost. I heaved a silent sigh of relief as we started communicating again.

As a youth, Bob said, he went to church and confession every week, and his parents provided him with a God-oriented world view. "My father was an amateur singer and actor," he said. "He told me I should make the best use of the abilities God had given me. After he died, I started to study singing, in part because that was what he had advised me to do. I thank God that he told me on his death bed, 'Don't waste a talent God has given you.'" Bob paused a moment, pondering those early days of his life, and then remarked, "I still remember one midnight mass that I attended with him. Some man got up to sing 'O Holy Night'—it was in French . . . we were French Catholics. My dad said he could do it better than that, and I recalled how well he had sung the same song a few years before at a mass. Well, I thought of my father two years ago when they asked me to sing 'O Holy Night' at the Bel Air Presbyterian Church. It was a unique experience for me. I said, 'This is for you, Dad,' and I sang the dickens out of it—a big high note that lasted forever."

The faith that Bob's family had inspired in him continued to influence him when he entered a conservatory in Toronto, and he was sometimes rather critical when his Catholic friends failed to attend services or observe some other ritual. "I'd say, 'How dare you! Don't you realize that's a sin?' I'd give them holy hell," he recalls.

But Bob reacted against his religious background when he and Carol Lawrence decided to get married in 1963. They approached church officials about being married in a Catholic ceremony but were rebuffed because Carol had been married previously in a Catholic church and the marriage had been annulled in a civil court. Although Bob had also been married and divorced, his wedding had taken place outside the church—"for reasons that are my own," he says. Under the church regulations he would have been permitted to be married as a Catholic, even though Carol was not.

"We were angry at the church, and I didn't attend services anywhere for four or five years," he said. "I didn't believe in anything. I was an agnostic. I didn't want to be bothered. I decided if that's the way the church handles its affairs, the heck with them. But as time went on, I realized it wasn't fair to the kids, not to know anything about God. We decided to give them some religious instruction. I called Pat Boone, my good friend and golfing buddy. He's a very religious man. He gave me three different churches, and one of them was Bel Air Presbyterian. I called the Reverend Don Moomaw there to see if it would be possible for my wife to come over to check about schooling for our children, and he said, 'What about you, Bob?' I told him politely I wasn't interested because I didn't really believe in anything. 'I'd like to have a talk with you,' he replied. But I said, 'We can talk, but it won't do you any good. My mind is made up.'"

Carol went on to a service with the kids and loved it. She was so enthusiastic that she finally talked Bob into attending. "When the morning came I didn't want to get out of bed, but Carol pleaded with me, so I said okay," he recalled. "I'd never been to a Protestant service before, but I really enjoyed myself. I'd never seen so many people smiling and happy."

Bob continued to attend the services whenever he was in California, and he sensed a gradual change taking place in his attitude toward God. Then one night he had a dream, which he described to Pat and Shirley Boone: "Last night, I dreamed I was dying," he told them. "And as I was about to die, I yelled out, 'Christ, save me!' Then I woke up and said to myself, 'You dummy! If you ask Him to save you while you're dying, why not ask Him to save you while you're still alive and well?'"

Bob's eyes misted as he remembered Shirley's reaction: "She started to cry and said, 'Praise the Lord!'"

The singer said his commitment came rather gradually as he tried to overcome his considerable skepticism about the church and Christian theology. He plied Don Moomaw with difficult questions about the faith, but finally decided that the only way he could learn whether the Christian position was valid was to begin to trust God in his daily life.

"God gave me a little push here, a little nudge there," Bob explained. "I needed something, but I didn't know what until the realization came upon me that it was faith. I didn't think I needed anything, but it's obvious now that I did. I thought I was self-sufficient, but just going to church, just being there, renewed something inside me. Some people need therapy or a psychiatrist, but I just talk to the man upstairs."

Some of the spiritual guidance he has received has come directly from Reverend Moomaw's pulpit: "In one of his sermons, Don said, 'Ask God in the name of Christ for something, and if it's not detrimental to you or anyone else, you'll receive it.' I said to myself, 'Oh, Don, that's a lot of malarkey!' But one day, when I needed something—not money or fame, but something to do with my work—I tried it. And it worked. It's worked on four different occasions."

Curious, I asked, "Do you recall what this thing was that you asked for?"

"Yes, but it's just a personal thing," Bob said. Perhaps because he senses he's still following Paul's admonition in Philippians 2:12 to "work out your own salvation with fear and trembling," Bob prefers not to discuss publicly many of his deepest spiritual feelings.

Television evangelist Rex Humbard had a similar reaction when I asked him during an interview for the *National Courier* whether he had ever had a Pentecostal experience such as speaking in tongues.

"Well, now, you're getting into personal things," Humbard replied. "And I would say to you that is a real nasty question that people shouldn't even be discussing. That's between me and the Lord."

Bob Goulet describes his own penchant for privacy this way: "I'm not a closet Christian, but I'm not going to prepare a twenty-minute speech and say, 'Friends, these are the spiritual insights I gained last week on my skiing trip when a ski pole went through my eye.' I'm still solidifying my spiritual position."

But I pressed him: "This thing you say you asked God for—was it an inner kind of need?"

"Yes—something I needed inside me, and God gave it to me," he replied tersely. "The answer I got was proof to me of God's presence."

But I still wasn't satisfied. "Now I don't want to push you into something you don't want to talk about, but was this like the peace that passes understanding that Paul talks about in his letter to the Philippians?"

"Not exactly," Bob replied. "It had to do with my work, but not any inner turmoil. It had to do with something in my work that I didn't have, that I needed. It has to do with peace in the framework of my labors. Now Christ and I talk every day. We have little conversations."

Some of those conversations with God occur just before Bob goes onstage for his nightclub act. "I don't pray all the time— just on special occasions," he told me. "But when I'm concerned for something, I say, 'Come on, Lord, hold my hand, here we go!' I ask Him for a helping hand, a shove if I start to fall. I think it's worked because I feel more confident."

I've always been fascinated by the question of which Person in the Trinity various Christians choose as the recipient of their prayers. Although some friends of mine feel comfortable talking to Jesus as though He were walking at their side, I myself usually just pray to God in general, as a vital personal presence, without considering whether the Father, the Son, or the

Holy Spirit is involved. When I asked Bob about his approach, he said, "Most of the time, I'm talking to Christ, because I know through Him I'll go to His Father, my Father. Sometimes I go right past Him, right past Kissinger to Ford, but most of the time I talk to Christ."

Bob's experiment in faith has prompted him to take some steps in his performances he would probably never have dreamed of taking before. For example, he occasionally injects a hymn or spiritual into his nightclub acts in Las Vegas, despite the fact that people in the audience sometimes snicker. He also accepted an invitation to perform on an Oral Roberts' Easter TV special. His moving rendition of the spiritual "Healing River" caused tears to well up in the eyes of many viewers, as well as in his own. "I have to get emotionally involved, and I'm afraid I do get choked up," he said, shaking his head. "That's stupid . . . I have to control myself."

My own experiences helped me identify with his problem. "I know the same feeling because I speak occasionally in front of groups about my faith," I said. "I get involved emotionally when I'm talking about things that are important to me, and I know it's hard . . ."

"You mustn't allow that to happen to you," he interjected, his professionalism now coming to the fore. "Of course, I cry when somebody drops a Kleenex," he said with a slight smile.

Bob summed up the core of his beliefs for me by referring with obvious affection, as he often does, to a family member: "My sister, a nun, gave me a crucifix she wore for years. I wear it around my neck most of the time now. I believe in the crucifix as well as the cross—that Christ died on the cross for my sins." It struck me as an interesting distinction, an insight apparently rooted as much in his Catholic cultural background as in his current personal beliefs.

"My decision to trust God has come slowly, but it is finally becoming cemented," he continued. "It's there now. I'm not the most holy of men—of course not. But I do believe in Christ, and I do believe in God. I do hope they'll forgive me my sins and take me in their arms when I cross the bar."

Bob is the first to admit that he faces many troublesome worldly obstacles, reminiscent of those that confronted Faithful and Christian as they visited Vanity Fair in John Bunyan's *The*

*Pilgrim's Progress.* The demands of his job and his fast-moving life-style constantly intrude to prevent him from following consistently the traditional paths of Christian spiritual growth, such as regular fellowship with other believers and Bible study. "I just don't have the time because I'm frequently out of town," he explained. "I spend less time in California than I do in Las Vegas. If I meet a Christian and he wants to talk about Christ or religion, I'll discuss it with him. Otherwise, I talk sports, or politics, or girls." He paused, then continued almost wistfully: "I do want to study the Bible. As a matter of fact, Don Moomaw gave me a modern version. But I have too many other things I have to read—affairs of the world and so forth."

My overall impression of Robert Goulet was that he's an intelligent man who still has many questions about what a relationship with Christ involves and what exactly God expects of him. But when the mood strikes him, he is more than willing to try some new thing that he feels may further his spiritual growth.

For example, part of becoming a Christian includes a public profession of faith, as the Apostle Paul says in Romans 10:9–10: ". . . if you confess with your lips that Jesus is Lord and believe in your heart that God raised him from the dead, you will be saved. For man believes with his heart and so is justified, and he confesses with his lips and so is saved." Goulet took this step one Sunday morning when he was attending Pat Boone's church, the Church on the Way, in Van Nuys, California. The pastor asked those who wanted to make a public affirmation of their faith to raise their hands, and Bob felt the pressure building up on him.

"I saw him looking at me four or five times, and finally I thought, 'I'll have to commit myself,'" Bob recalls. "But I debated the issue for a few moments. 'He wants me to commit myself, but I *already* have,' I thought. 'I don't have to put my hand up to talk to the Lord.' But finally I did raise my hand. Before you know it, the pastor said, 'All those who raised their hands, please stay after the service and come to the room at the back of the sanctuary.' They talked to us back there for about a half hour on the meaning of a Christian commitment and gave us some literature to read."

After this service, Goulet's natural curiosity about unfamiliar

Christian practices came to the surface when a strange woman walked up to him and said, "Oh, praise the Lord! Have you had the blessing of the tongues yet?"

"The what?" he retorted. After a brief conversation, he still couldn't figure out what place speaking in tongues, or glossolalia, might have in a Christian's spiritual experience. In recounting the incident to me, he looked me directly in the eye and asked, "Is it true people do talk in other tongues, without any prior knowledge of the language?"

I was somewhat taken aback because when I'm conducting an interview, I'm not used to being asked serious factual questions—especially not by a celebrity. But Bob Goulet is a very inquisitive man, and I knew he wouldn't be satisfied until he had an adequate answer.

"Are you asking me?" I said, just to be sure I'd heard correctly.

"Yes."

"As a matter of fact," I said, "I was reading Pat Boone's autobiography, *A New Song,* the other day, and I understand his wife prays partially in Latin—a language she's never been taught. When I've heard people speaking in tongues, though, it's not a language anyone could translate. It's a very fluent kind of thing that may involve different sounds, depending on the individual."

"Are you in a trance-like state?" he pressed, now on the edge of his chair. "Or can you make it happen at will?"

"I've had an experience similar to this myself," I admitted, deciding that the time had come to open up completely to him. "With me, it's not the kind of thing I can turn on. It comes to me when I'm in a particular frame of mind. If I want to pray to God in a certain way, I may not be able to articulate my thoughts in ordinary language. The sounds come from inside me and express feelings I can't put into words."

"Do you speak like this with someone else around?"

"No. I never do it with anyone else around. A lot of people do it in groups, but I never have. I don't feel comfortable that way."

Bob pondered this for a moment and then asked, "As the sounds come out of you, you don't understand the precise

96

translation, but you do know the central meaning of what you're saying?"

"I know the impression, the general import," I explained.

"Hmmmm," he murmured thoughtfully.

"I didn't think I'd ever get involved in this sort of thing because I tend to be too reserved—but it happened," I added.

"I know it'll scare the daylights out of me if it ever happens to me!" he replied. "I'll say, 'Carol, Carol, come and listen to this!'"

We both laughed, and he sat back as I poured another cup of coffee. His casual, affectionate references to Carol Lawrence were typical of him. In retrospect, it's amazing to me that he was able to talk so positively about her when only a few weeks later she filed for legal separation. It was almost as though he wasn't aware that his marriage was crumbling. In fact, he told me that their mutual Christian faith had brought them closer together with a new warmth and understanding. And he mused contentedly about a vacation they had planned to their country home in Jackson Hole, Wyoming.

When I talked to Carol Lawrence the next morning, I didn't get quite as positive a view of their marriage. It's not that she said anything overtly critical of their relationship. It's just that while Bob was jealously protective of many aspects of his private life, including some of his religious views, she was completely open about a number of the problems they faced.

I arrived a little early, and she greeted me in a pink housecoat and long, flowing black hair. But even in this conventional housewife's garb, Carol somehow seemed regal and sophisticated. After ushering me into their expansive French Provincial living room and offering me a seat near a huge grand piano, she immediately offered me some coffee. I sensed, in her warmth and graciousness, that Carol was interested in relating to me as a human being and also, more importantly, as a fellow Christian. Unlike many famous performers, she had called me herself the previous day to set up the interview, without going through any agent or public relations representative. Here was a woman who obviously knew how to operate without a passel of maids and servants, even though she could well have afforded them.

Bob had apparently warned her about my temperamental tape recorder because she asked me politely if it was working all right, or if I'd prefer that she bring theirs in again.

I assured her it was working but said, "I can't figure what was wrong yesterday. It was strange."

In marked contrast to Bob's impatience, she said softly, "They do that, you know. I can't explain it, but sometimes mine is that way. You have to kind of talk to it nicely."

I laughed and confessed, "I prayed over it this morning."

"Yes, that's the second thing you have to do," she said, smiling. Any feelings of discomfort or nervousness I may have had about the interview had disappeared. Presumptuous as it might sound, I quickly realized that Carol Lawrence was my Christian sister.

Carol's life has always involved some tension between her stage career and her religious instincts. This inner struggle emerged clearly at the outset of our conversation. She said, "I was brought up as a strict Italian Roman Catholic and went through all the wonderful [religious] stages. I even thought about becoming a nun. But I always sang and danced—that was an instinctive thing with me. I really needed to perform more than I needed to become a nun."

Recalling Bob's early thoughts about the priesthood, I was struck with how similar their background influences were. Their marriage seemed like such a perfect match as I listened to her. During her childhood, she continued, her mother and father had been deeply involved in the religious life of the Chicago suburb where they lived. During one of the community's major Catholic festival parades, for example, Carol recalled, "My mother would carry candles and walk barefoot through the streets of the town—as a sacrifice for whatever gifts she had received from God. My father was always one of the 'Holy Name Selected Few' who actually carried a life-size statue of the Madonna and Child on his shoulders, with several other men. My mother had to put a towel on his shoulder so it wouldn't be bruised.

"So you see, my background is really deeply rooted in religion. And I was happy as a bug in my relationship to Christ. But I never was overjoyed at the treatment I got from the nuns or priests, and I never felt a joyous camaraderie in the congregation. Mass was always obligatory, as was not eating meat on Friday. You were born to love and serve God, but I never sensed God showing love for me from His direction."

Carol showed early promise as a singer and dancer, and the first years of her show business career moved along like a storybook plot. She entered Northwestern University on a full scholarship and was voted "Freshman of the Year" in the theater department. Then in a fateful move, she visited New York City with her family during the summer vacation before her sophomore year. It was natural for the budding performer to want to check out the Broadway theater scene, so she decided to sit in on a play audition to see what it would be like. When the open call for dancers began, though, she was told she could only watch if she was a participant herself. So she dressed up in rehearsal clothes, lined up with the other dancers, and landed her first professional job.

During this period, she says, she was "exposed to religious questions for the first time: 'Why is the Pope infallible? Why do you believe in the Immaculate Conception of Mary?' Everybody conversed freely about everything. I was the only Catholic in a mostly Jewish show. I was exposed to homosexuals, all sorts of people. It was all very stimulating, exciting, and I wanted to know more about my religion, to dig deeper."

But when she returned home during the first break in her schedule, she found that she had grown beyond her background. "I wanted to share my questions about religion with my family, but they were terribly upset that I would think about such things. I knew I couldn't pursue the subject without hurting them, so I swallowed it. I never really got the answers I wanted. It was my own fault because I didn't have the time to study theology. So I found myself slipping away from the religion of my childhood."

When Carol returned to New York City, she became worried that her family might put pressure on her to return home permanently. "I wanted to stay in New York, but there seemed to be a feeling at home that if a girl lives alone in New York, she can't earn a decent living. She would have to become a prostitute or be exposed to other evils and lose her soul in the process.

"Then, at age eighteen, I met a man who was a television

puppeteer, an Italian Catholic, and I thought he was a very nice person. After I had known him for two weeks, we became engaged. I had to return to Chicago for a three-month engagement, and I thought this would put everybody back home at ease. Now I had this protector in New York, and I expected we'd be engaged for two or three years and get married if it worked out. I knew I didn't know him that well.

"Unfortunately, he insisted that I marry him immediately. He felt if I became successful, I would not stay with him, so we were married while I was still eighteen. It was the worst mistake that any young person can make. I was in a marriage that I knew, three weeks later, was never going to work. But in my life at that time divorce did not exist. It was not in my vocabulary. And I couldn't admit to everybody so quickly that I had made a bad choice. It was a youthful, stupid mistake."

Despite her unhappy first marriage, Carol experienced spectacular success in her career. She appeared on Broadway in major roles in *Shangri-La* and the *Ziegfeld Follies* of 1957, and landed the coveted role of Maria in *West Side Story* after surviving thirteen auditions and outshining thousands of other actresses who wanted the part. She was established as a major star after *West Side Story,* but her marriage was still in trouble.

"I was exposed to living agony, day in and day out," she told me bitterly. "I lived through that for three years, until I just could not look myself in the face any more. I said I wanted out, and he said he would never give me a divorce."

An annulment was finally arranged, but it was not recognized by Carol's church, and she consequently became disillusioned with organized religion. "I still have a scar which hasn't healed completely. The experience did absolutely nothing to my attitude toward Christ, but I lived in the Land of Nod after this for [several] years. I didn't go to church at all. I still performed on Broadway, on television, and in the movies, and I made recording albums. I threw myself overzealously into my work, to get over the pain of it all."

After the annulment, Carol considered herself a Christian, but "it was a private kind of thing. My prayer was far more personal, not organized. But I never felt forsaken by Christ. That would have killed me."

"Did you ever question whether God was there?" I asked.

"Oh, no! I think I would have fallen apart!" she exclaimed. "What did you pray for?"

"Many things," she replied. "My mother has always been a person with health problems. I prayed for her and for my father. I could see answers to prayer when I was depressed, or when things looked bad for me. It was always a comfort for me to know Christ was there. It was an emotional healing experience."

She and Robert Goulet met in 1961 when they were cast as husband and wife in *The Enchanted Nutcracker,* a musical special on television. They were married in 1963. Although they were unable to get married inside the Catholic church because of Carol's prior marriage, she didn't react bitterly into agnosticism as Bob did. "I had dealt with that problem already. It didn't do anything to me; it wasn't a surprise. We spoke little about religion. In the first years of marriage, we had no communication on a spiritual level."

Carol admits that she went to the Bel Air Presbyterian Church in the early 1970s because she felt her two sons needed religious instruction. But there was also "a tremendous need in me too," she admitted. "I think by that time I really wanted some answers and needed a kind of nurturance. I think there was a great deal missing in my life."

I understood what she was talking about because my own faith runs into "zero growth" periods during which, for one reason or another, I'm not as close to God as I should be. "Are you saying your faith had progressed to a certain level, but somehow you couldn't go beyond that point—your spiritual growth was sort of stunted?" I asked.

"Right, exactly," she agreed. "I really had more of a need for Christ in my life. I needed to have Him take a bigger part in my activities because my responsibilities were greater. I had two children to try to help along the way, and I really needed help. So I turned to Him. Yes, it's becoming clearer to me now. I was looking for an excuse to fulfill my own need. God used my relationship with my children to help me personally. I could easily have sent them to church with the nurse if that had been all I wanted."

Carol went to Bel Air Presbyterian Church alone with the kids because Bob, as he indicated earlier, wasn't interested himself. "It was a wonderful experience," she recalled. "The service was so beautiful, and everything about it was directed to today's needs, to the person living in the chaotic hostilities that we have to cope with. No demands were made on me, no guilt was preached, everything was joyous. For the first time, I got the message that God loves the people, in addition to requiring love Himself. When I left the service, someone handed me a weekly prayer suggestion, and I was invited to go out onto a patio for some coffee with other members of the congregation.

"One woman walked up to me and asked, 'How are you?' She held my hand, looked into my eyes—it was really a revelation. She *really* wanted to know how I was."

"Did she know you were Carol Lawrence?" I asked.

"No, not at all. She just asked, 'Are you okay? Can I help you?' At the end of every service, the pastor says, 'Turn and greet the person next to you.' It really works, helps you take off your little blindfolds."

"What about Bob?" I wondered. "When did he start attending?"

"It took me a long time to get my husband to come up to the church," she said. "He just didn't want to be bothered. I finally said, 'Bobby, you have to come to see the service, meet Don, and see that the kids are well cared for.' He did finally come up and he was really floored, really loved it. He started going regularly when he was in town."

Although her spiritual renewal began at this point, a year or two passed before Carol got involved in a small fellowship group with other Christian women. She finally found—as I have in my own spiritual trek—that regular interaction with other believers is a must for Christian growth. "Fellowship groups, that sort of thing, didn't exist in my background," she explained. "Plus, I'm constantly running and dashing. My life has always been pretty much a running race. I finally joined a group of eight or ten women, organized by Carol Moomaw, and I learned so much and got so much support. We shared with each other, dealt with personal problems. And we would read from Bible passages and engage in conversational prayer. That was hard for me because I'd never in my life prayed out loud.

"But it was a tremendous experience for me. By sharing my

joys and sorrows and problems, by reaching out and trying to help another person in a loving way, I was drawn closer to Christ, closer to the suffering He had. Understanding His human qualities made me feel closer to Him and more worthy of His love. I found in that sort of sisterhood there was a tremendous nourishing of my own spiritual growth."

A couple of years later, Carol switched to another small Christian prayer group, which was led by the former dancer Marge Champion. She also decided to cement her ties with her church by enrolling in a ten-week membership course, which required her to "examine personal relationships, write a report on where I was as a Christian. This was so enlightening, so informative as we met in a small group of seven or eight people. We became so close—as I have found happens in many small fellowship groups."

An interesting change occurred in her approach to her career as a result of this close-knit membership class. "I was asked to co-host the 1975 Cerebral Palsy Telethon during the time I was attending the class. My involvement with the church group prompted me to do something different: I went down to the cerebral palsy center and talked to the therapists and the children. I had learned that Christ said if we give love, it will be returned to us. To give love is to receive it. And I found, after co-hosting and performing for nineteen hours on that program, I had more strength and was happier, healthier, and feeling better than at any time I can remember."

Interested in what practical impact her Christian renewal had made on her professional life, I said, "By the way, a friend of mine—a Harvard psychologist I'm writing a book with—said he'd heard you, in some Chicago nightclub, singing religious songs as part of your act. Is that right?"

"Yes, I constructed a new act which opens with a spiritual—'Any Friend of the Father Is a Good, Good Friend of Mine'—and it really rocks!" she exclaimed, clapping her hands and snapping her fingers. "I sing, 'I'm so happy to be here among you, sharing thoughts with those who feel the way I do, and it thrills me so to join in the proclaiming of the joy that has united me and you.' You can't listen to it without tapping your toes!"

Caught up in her description and literally about to explode

with song, she almost seemed to forget I was sitting there listening: "I close with a medley of Gospel songs, like 'A . . . a . . . men! Aaaa . . . men!'" she continued, singing pieces of the melodies and, in effect, giving me an impromptu performance in her living room. "This kind of thing is recent for me, and it arises directly out of my own spiritual renewal," she noted.

Carol went on to describe enthusiastically the Christian musical ministry she was developing—which included a new religious album, concerts at churches, and witnessing about her faith on secular television programs. But I sensed, in the midst of all this happiness and satisfaction, that there were also a few problems in her life. Specifically, I had read in one gossip column that there were rumors of troubles in her relationship with Bob. I wanted to know whether or not her Christian faith, which had undergone a rejuvenation through close relationships with other believers, was also helping her wrestle with any current marital problems. Deciding to approach the question indirectly—as I would with any Christian neighbor who might not want me meddling in her private business—I asked, "You know, it's obvious you're talented and attractive. Do you find many people looking at you and saying, 'She doesn't need anything. She's got it all, with a career and home like this. She's self-sufficient, without any problems'?"

"One close friend always thinks that about me, until he comes into this house and sees its utter chaos," she replied with a sigh. "We live a very hectic, difficult life. I'm married to someone with a successful career who is away a lot of the time. And I try to maintain the semblance of a career too. Mine always takes second place because I feel our home comes first. That is something I have to deal with on a personal level because I've not reached a point where I can truthfully say I'll give up my career and devote my life to sitting at home, doing all the housewifely and motherly things. I enjoy those things, but I can't say I'll never go back on the stage again. It would be hypocritical because I would eventually become very resentful."

"Have you found your mutual spiritual commitment—yours and Bob's—has helped you balance any conflicts you feel in your marriage relationship?"

"Yes. People always say, 'Isn't it hard being married to such a handsome man? He's always on the road, and all the women are running after him. And isn't it a problem when you're working together, with the competition?' I always say, 'No, it's easy.'" She paused slightly and then continued more quietly. "But it's not easy. It's not easy at all. Except if you say it's not easy, then wonderful people like Rona Barrett and all those rag magazines say, 'Oh, Carol Lawrence says it's terrible being married to Robert Goulet!' And all I said is, it's difficult."

Now that the door to the subject was open, I forged ahead: "As a matter of fact, I saw something in a gossip column that said the Goulet-Lawrence marriage is in trouble," I said.

"That's been going on for twelve years now."

"You mean your marriage has been in trouble for that long?" I said, laughing to let her know I was joking.

"No, no," she replied. "But it's a difficult thing to maintain. I think marriage is a difficult thing for anyone—for a plumber and his wife or whoever. But in our situation everything is compounded. To say problems didn't exist was my way of being defensive so that the interviewer didn't ask the next question: 'What *are* the problems?' If I said we had a problem, the columnist would immediately focus on the negative [side of our relationship]. It's far more juicy for someone to speculate, 'Oh, does Robert Goulet cheat? Wow!' Rather than have that, I try to always give a positive response.

"That little rumor [about marital problems] has been going around for months and months now. It was based on the fact that we had a terrible argument in Las Vegas. That was a very difficult period, and we very nearly called it quits. To say my spiritual commitment has helped would have to be absolutely true because otherwise I think I would have said forget it ages ago."

As she spoke, I found myself comparing her situation with my own marriage, so I asked, "Have you reached the stage where you and Bob can pray together? The reason I ask is that in my marriage, it took a long time before my wife and I could do that."

"No, we've not gotten to that position yet," Carol said. "He feels sometimes my church group is changing me in a way that would take me away. We would stay up [at night] and he would insist that I give him definite proof of God's existence, because there is no question in my mind that there is a God

105

and a Christ, and that He works in my life. He couldn't have a child who was a cripple. [He says,] 'Why is there starving in Bangladesh? Why are they fighting in Ireland and killing each other?' I say, 'I can't give you an answer to that. That's man's choice, and if he chooses not to obey God or do His work, then you mustn't blame Christ for that.' We would stay up until six o'clock in the morning. He would be screaming and pounding and yelling. So we've not come anywhere near praying together. I pray for that day. It would be tremendous."

Such disagreements about the faith are by no means unheard of between Christian husbands and wives, especially when both are as thoughtful and independently minded as Carol and Bob. But apparently their problems ran deeper than I realized, for I was shocked and saddened when I heard on the radio about a month later that they had separated shortly after I had talked with them. Carol had petitioned for legal separation and asked for custody of their two sons, according to a Los Angeles *Times* story. Both she and Bob had been so personable and kind to me that it almost seemed that two of my Christian friends were splitting and that any possibility for me to relate to them together in the future, as one in Christ, had been lost. Professionally, they were made for each other. In such productions as *Camelot* at the Dorothy Chandler Pavilion in Los Angeles, they broke all attendance records. But somehow their separate spiritual pilgrimages had not meshed, and the personal side of their relationship ran into trouble. I pray that whatever the precise problems that have estranged them, they may find a way through Christ to heal their misunderstandings.

Chapter 8

# *Capital Faith*

## SENATOR MARK HATFIELD
## AND CHARLES COLSON

As Senator Mark Hatfield finished a phone call, I stared at a plaque over his office door, which bore the inscription "Chemeketa." It was one of the few mementoes and emblems on the walls that didn't refer to Abraham Lincoln. I suspected it must be some sort of Indian term that had special significance for him, so when the Oregon Republican finished his conversation, and swung his chair around to face me, I asked, "What's that word up there?"

"It comes from the language of the Chinook tribe," he explained. "It means 'A place of peace.'"

Peace. It was the kind of code word that liberal politicians and antiwar activists had always seemed to like. Evangelical politicians, many of whom are conservatives, usually seem to favor words like "patriotism" and "free enterprise." But of course I knew Hatfield wasn't the usual Evangelical politician. He had been an outspoken critic of the war in Vietnam and was one of the leaders in Congress in the attack on world hunger. Despite his meticulous, well-groomed, conservative appearance, Hatfield was, in many ways, a maverick, and I wanted to find out what made him tick.

"I notice you have quite a few pictures of Abraham Lincoln," I said. "Is he one of your favorite people?"

"You might gather that, since the walls are literally covered with prints, photos, mementoes, and symbols of Lincoln," he replied rather formally. "Yes, I have a great interest in Lincoln. He was a man with a great sensitivity to human beings. He's one of the most well-rounded public servants we've ever had in this country. He was politically astute and pragmatic, yet he had this deep philosophical undergirding. He ran totally counter to the understanding which prevails today of leadership and power. We have come to define power as the capacity to dominate, manipulate, and persuade to a particular point of view. But Mr. Lincoln felt his power was in the tradition of the servant leader. He wanted to persuade, yes, but not dominate and manipulate. It was not an ego-denigrating type of power which drove him to sustain his own career at the cost of other people."

Hatfield's speech was as well organized as his office, but he seemed a little standoffish and reserved. I got the impression that he was measuring his words carefully until he had sized me up. He knew I was a writer, but I suspected he was unsure about the purpose of my visit. I had written him that I was working on a book about Christian conversions and renewals, but I knew I hadn't stated my own faith position clearly.

"Maybe I should mention that the main thing I'm interested in discussing is your Christian experiences," I said. "I'm a Christian myself, by the way."

He relaxed visibly, and a friendly, intimate smile appeared on his lips. "Oh . . ." he said. "You're writing from some perspective."

"That's right," I replied. "I'm not questioning the fact that God acts in people's lives. I'm just trying to find exactly how He has worked through certain individuals and how he leads others to Himself. I noticed in your book, *Conflict and Conscience,* that you mentioned you underwent a conversion experience when you were thirty-one years old. I'd like to go into that more deeply."

Speaking more personally now, the Senator said, "I'd say more accurately it was a renewal. I had an authentic conversion experience when I was a boy about thirteen. But the relevance and reality of a relationship with Christ on a day-to-day basis was not something I fully comprehended—or made myself vulnerable for—until I was in my professional life. As a counselor of students, I learned from my students. This renewal came through the witness and changed lives I observed on campus at Williamette University in Oregon."

"Do you think you had a personal relation with Christ when you were a boy?"

"I find the more I delve into the Scripture, the more I'm persuaded the Gospel I accepted as a boy was a doctrine or dogma. It was never personified. I now see the Gospel as a person, and I do feel the relational concept [to the person, Christ] was missing in my first commitment."

I wondered whether his early religious Christian experience was similar to the experiences of those whom Paul criticized in 2 Timothy 3:5 for "holding the form of religion but denying the power of it."

"Yes," he agreed. "I could cite the catechism quite easily: the deity of Christ, blood atonement, inspiration of Scripture, Second Advent. I never questioned those. But to take those beliefs and appropriate them to my life-style, my value system— an abandonment and commitment to Christ, the energy and power that comes out of a trust relationship—I don't think that became a reality until later. I was an institutional or acculturated Christian. My life-style didn't reflect anything distinctive."

Hatfield explained that he was reared in a Baptist church environment, "which was highly legalistic. Your badge was that you didn't smoke, drink, go to movies, dance, or go with girls who did. Well, I did all and enjoyed all. To me, Christianity was a matter of having to give up things to follow Christ, when really it's not that at all. But that's the way I understood it because it was being preached that way."

His affirmation of the forms of cultural Christianity persisted into his service in the Navy during World War II. He said he and his military buddies on occasion headed toward the officers' club "to tie one on. We'd usually have three subjects we discussed: politics, religion, and sex, in that order. In the religious discussion, I would identify myself as a fundamentalist, though I hate the word now. I would defend all the tenets of the faith, and my friends would always say, 'Why, if you're a fundamentalist, why are you drinking?' I'd say, 'I'm a fundamentalist theologically, but not in social practice.' I'd rationalize and separate my life into different compartments.

"I also conducted religious services on Sundays when there was no chaplain on the ship. A Catholic officer did the same for the Catholics, and we'd have a little competition. I think God used that experience, because I found my relationship to enlisted people really changed. They began to share their personal problems, and I became deeply concerned about them. It gave me my first experience in teaching and professional counseling."

Hatfield remained a cultural Christian after his release from the service, but his lack of a deep faith didn't hinder the meteoric rise of his career. He became the dean of students and professor of political science at Willamette University and was also elected to the state legislature at age twenty-eight.

"Did you feel any need to search for a deeper understanding of God?" I asked.

"No," he said emphatically. "I was very self-sufficient."

Comparing his pre-Christian experiences with mine, I remarked, "In my own case, my parents' faith was my faith. But in my last year in high school, I began to doubt very seriously that there was a God. That led me into a search to find out if there really was a Supreme Being."

He shook his head. "I always assumed there was a God—never went through an agnostic or atheistic period. I had no problem with the Trinity either—always accepted it."

"That's interesting," I mused. "I searched for God, and He convinced me one night that He was really there. But I know a lot of people take the route you took. In your case, it wasn't so much disbelieving in Christ as deciding to follow Him."

"My problem was indifference, and I believe there's nothing worse than being indifferent," the Senator declared. "In a way, I think it's easier to handle doubt than indifference. I went through this whole worship of intellectualism. You usually think of intellectuals as being anti-God, but I never had that problem. I just accepted Christianity at a young age, and was so acculturated that doubts about God's existence never really entered my mind. I guess some might say I was an extreme Calvinist. I had made my decision, so now I could go out and raise hell."

110

"But you said it was some of your students who made you change your way of thinking?" I asked.

"Yes. They began to come into my office to share some of their personal problems—you know, 'What is life all about?' and so on. I began to realize that the political philosophy I was expounding in my classroom [did not automatically answer] questions relating to a personal philosophy of life. And I felt most deficient there [in the area of personal philosophy]. I began to do some introspective thinking because I always wanted to feel very assured about things."

"How did you answer them when they asked you about your philosophy of life?"

"I would give them a humanistic generality," Hatfield said. "But I realized I wasn't saying much when I'd tell them, 'We should all try to work together to make a better world, respect each other, have understanding of our differences. Our American society is a great mosaic having various hues and shades and colors, and this is the beauty of America which we need to see in our daily lives. If we can work through the United Nations to help bring understanding to all people of the world . . .'" Then he stopped and smiled at me. "It was so much hogwash. Each time I said things like that to students, I felt I had been shoveling empty words at them. I didn't feel it."

But then he met a student named Doug Coe, whose mother had been Hatfield's Sunday School teacher. "He wanted to get my approval to establish a chapter of the Intervaristy Christian Fellowship on campus, and he asked if I would come and speak at one of their meetings and become their adviser."

Though somewhat unsure about this turn of events, Dean Hatfield nevertheless agreed, and he soon found himself dealing with a steady stream of Christian luminaries who came in to speak to the students: Bill Bright of Campus Crusade; Carl F. H. Henry, then a professor at Fuller Seminary; leaders of the Navigators and Young Life. "They were parading through my office, and I was impressed," he recalled. "They were concentrated on this person of Christ, yet they were very normal-acting. Nobody sniffed the air because I was smoking, or looked down their noses at me because of this or that. I was really quite impressed with the students as well as the speakers."

Two students came to his office one day and said they

111

wanted to share a recent experience with him: "They said they had accepted Christ as their Lord and Savior, and I said, 'That's nice.' I thought there must have been a tent meeting somewhere nearby and I sort of passed them off down the sawdust trail. But it really began to bother me when I heard these students were leading a Bible study at a fraternity house. That was totally contrary to the campus mores at this time [the early 1950s]. I knew these kids well, and I saw them having an impact by leading a different, totally different life-style. An almost minirevival was occurring at that campus, and that was having an impact on me.

"At first, I sort of put it off. I thought it was a passing thing. Then I became curious, then it bothered me, then it hit me. It was a cumulative thing, the result of various exposures to different Christian people, listening to them and seeing their lives change. And there was the persistence of people like Doug Coe, a very charismatic person. They had been praying for me, though I didn't know it. They weren't grabbing me by the lapel and asking if I'd be saved—that would have turned me around."

The way that Senator Hatfield became a Christian reminded me of Pat Boone's story of his own conversion. "My decision was completely rational, not emotional," the Senator said. "It was very pragmatic. I came to the place where I said, 'Lord, I've either got to get on, or get off. I've been living my life with my ego, my desire for a political career. I can't really call myself a follower of Christ without displacing my ego with You.' I felt miserable because I had been living a schizophrenic life. It was a dichotomy I couldn't handle. Finally I said, 'I'm going to commit my life to You and see where we go.'"

Soon after making this private commitment, Senator Hatfield met with several of the Christian students he knew and prayed with them. "That was the first time I'd prayed with anyone else like that, and I felt at ease sharing my commitment. I was thirty-two years old at the time of this renewal—it was in the early 1950s."

"Did you find your way of life changed after your commitment?" I asked.

"It wasn't that I was living a raunchy kind of life of sin," he replied. "The changes that occurred were evolutionary. I began

112

to study the Word deeply, prayed each day. Then I had to face up to certain social practices in which I was engaged. I began to see them as crutches I had used, such as having to hold on to a pipe, a cigar, a cigarette, or a Scotch and soda. I made a decision not to drink or smoke, because I was afraid my practices might provide a problem or stumbling block for the other person. I could have a Scotch and soda today, and it would have no effect on my faith. And I refuse to accept abstention as a badge of Christianity. But [at the time] I had to be honest with myself: Did these things contribute to, or hinder, my spiritual development? I had to conclude that they were hindering it. In other words, at a cocktail party, I should be able to communicate Christ without a glass. As for smoking, I had felt there was a certain social acceptance I'd gain by smoking. But if Christ is sufficient for all our needs, then I should not have need of these things to give me assurance."

Mark Hatfield was married to his wife, Antoinette, when he was thirty-five. He fathered four children and went on to become governor and U. S. Senator from Oregon. His faith continued to influence him, not only in his private life but in his public career as well. He seemed quite comfortable using his faith as a moral foundation to build enthusiastic policy positions on national and international issues, and I admired him for this ability because I often found I was unable to work up much enthusiasm over such topics. Take the problem of world hunger, for example. My inability to get excited about starvation and malnutrition had been bothering me for quite a while, and I told him so.

"There's one thing I think maybe you can help me with," I began. "I recently decided to try to bring my writing files up to date. As I spent the last three or four days working on them, I noticed that by far and away the largest number of newspaper clips I had collected were on world hunger and the population crisis. God seemed to be saying something to me through my voluminous collection of these materials. I've often said I'm not by nature a very altruistic person, though God has helped me in terms of dealing with individuals—He encourages me to visit sick acquaintances in hospitals and so forth. But I have never been able to transfer this concern for private individuals to global issues. Somehow, I don't seem to have the strong

113

compassionate feelings that you do. Can you give me any advice on how I can move in your direction?"

Hatfield thought for a moment and then replied, "I think we all carry certain characteristics from our cultural and environmental backgrounds. When I was a boy, I can vividly remember the Depression. My father worked three days a week on the railroad, and my mother taught school. I had aunts and uncles and cousins with no jobs. We would gather together, pick vegetables, and can them for the whole family in Oregon. We even took one of my cousins to live with us so that the need in that particular family would be relieved. Also, there were people who traveled the rails and knocked on our door, six or eight of them a day, and my parents never turned them away. They'd have to work first—maybe split some wood for us. That was my parents' ethic. But my background impressed me indelibly with the idea that we are to share with people who are in need.

"Then I have traveled extensively to many parts of the world and seen hunger and poverty there," he continued. "Outside of my own bedroom, the times when I've become the most emotional have been when I've seen abject poverty. I've visited Mother Teresa in Calcutta and a Palestinian refugee camp in Jordan. I've walked through the ghetto here in Washington in a pair of wash pants with a Vista worker. I didn't go as a Senator —no cameras or newspapers to travel along and exploit the poor as I got my picture taken. It was just a matter of walking in as a friend, and having little babies and children reach up to you.

"I can weep in an orphanage. I have wept. Tears have come to my eyes, and I've had to brush them away. I'm a visual person, and I have to see things firsthand. But I don't think that even the most jaded person could leave Calcutta without being moved—provided that he gets outside his room at the Grand Hotel. You have to see a person dying on the street, lying there like so much garbage. Or you see Mother Teresa picking up elderly people off the street, cradling their heads when they have only about an hour to live. She says no one should die without having love and hearing about Jesus.

"These are the things that have led me to personalize my position on world hunger. I can still see the people with their hands held out. These images fit naturally into my faith, and remind me of what Jesus said in Matthew 25: ". . . for I was hungry and you gave me food, I was thirsty and you gave me drink . . . as you did it to one of the least of these my brethren, you did it to me."

Mark Hatfield obviously felt strongly about this issue because he spoke with an intensity that hadn't been evident in our previous conversation. "There's such hard evidence in Scripture that compassion for others is an affirmation of our faith in Him," he continued. "The emphasis shouldn't be just on statistical conversions. We don't have any evidence that everybody Christ blessed or fed believed in Him. Providing for the physical needs of others is an independent responsibility, apart from conversion. We're called to be agents of reconciliation, for the body and the soul. Christ exercised His great healing powers toward the sick, the lame, the blind, and the hungry. If we really believe Christ died for us while we were yet sinners—and saved us by that unmerited favor we call grace—do we have any right to demand that anyone else in the human family must *earn* the right for us to love them? Grace is a continuing thing, an energizing force. I feel that since we didn't earn Christ's love, we can't demand that other people earn our love." Looking at me squarely, he declared, "As a Christian, I have an unlimited liability for your well-being."

Senator Hatfield sounded more like a theologian than a politician as he described his views on world hunger. I began to wonder how he reconciled his faith with some of the more unseemly aspects of politics, such as the temptation to compromise principle and the frequent corruption of character by power. Was it possible that God had actually led him into the political arena? "Did you feel a call to public life after your renewal experience?" I asked.

"No, I didn't, and I'd be very reluctant to say now that I'm called. I'd say I'm called as of today, but to say I'm called by God as of tomorrow—I don't know. I think one plays with fire if he develops a Messianic complex. William Jennings Bryan said he was called to be President of the United States, but after the votes were counted, God lost. I'm not going to put God in that position.

"I *can't* lose an election. My opponent may get more votes, but I still win because my commitment is to God's will. It's obvious to me that if an opponent gets more votes, God has some other place for me. Therefore, I'm still the winner in seeking God's will. That's the only belief that keeps me from climbing the walls in this jungle: I don't have to worry about the next election."

"You know, I was telling a friend of mine that I'd be talking with you, and he said, 'Gee, I wish that guy would run for President!' Do you have any thoughts in that direction now?" I asked.

"No, I don't," he said emphatically. "I *have* had in the past, but . . ." and then he hesitated. "No, there are some things that don't make me feel safe and secure. I don't like to entertain that idea [being President]. I deliberately try to keep it out of my mind. I've seen it destroy people. I know what a narcotic it can become, how you can lose perspective. I think I could handle the thought of becoming President, but I don't dwell on it. Then, I face the reality that it just can't happen to people like me—without the Lord's miracle. First of all, I'm not a wealthy person, and [the presidential campaign] is becoming increasingly the business of wealthy people or those who have access to wealth. I'm not poor-mouthing, but I have neither."

As he pondered the subject, though, other possibilities came to his mind. "If you move through succession—if you were Vice-President and follow when the President steps aside—you can move up that ladder. That would be more realistic for a person in my position. I did entertain that at one time. I was supposed to be a finalist for the vice-presidency in 1968 in the mind of Richard Nixon, and the Lord spared me from that. I gave it some thought then. I made [my positions part of the public] record so people would know my views. I was evidently felt out about that by Mr. Knight of the Knight newspapers. I was asked to have lunch with him in Miami, and as we ate, his afternoon newspaper came out with the headline 'Nixon-Hatfield Ticket Predicted.' That's pretty heady stuff, and Mr. Knight said, 'What would you think about that?' I said, 'That depends. It depends on the kinds of compromises I have to make. I refuse to compromise on issues I feel very strongly about—namely, the war [in Vietnam] for one thing. If

116

it were offered to me contingent upon my abandonment of my principles, then no.'"

The offer of the vice-presidency in that year went to Spiro Agnew, of course, and the rest is history. I couldn't argue with Hatfield's decision on the vice-presidency, but I found myself wondering if he might not be a little too rigid, too unwilling to compromise. "Would your emphasis on certain principles shift according to the main public issues of the day?" I asked.

"Yes," he said. "But at no point in my political life would I be willing to abandon or sacrifice my *basic* commitments or principles for political events. As a consequence I can sleep at night."

As I pondered his 1968 decision to turn down the vice-presidency, I suddenly remembered that as a Marine Corps officer-lawyer in 1968, I had corresponded with him. "When I was a judge advocate in the Marines, I drafted a letter advocating a form of universal service, and I got several other Marine lawyers to sign it. We sent you a copy, and you wrote a personal reply disagreeing with us. But I don't guess you'd remember . . ."

"Yes, I *do* remember," he said. "We were fighting the draft then, to get it abolished."

"As I look back on myself in those days, I think I was probably less sensitive on some issues then than I feel I am now," I mused. "But I'm curious. Suppose you had just come out of law school and were confronted with having to enter the military during the Vietnam war. What would you have done?"

"I was in college when Pearl Harbor was bombed," Senator Hatfield replied. "When we were attacked, I marched down with everyone else. But I'm fully persuaded I could never have joined, nor have permitted myself to yield to military service during the Vietnam War."

"If you had been a lawyer, you'd still have refused to be inducted? You know that would mean you'd have had a conviction on your record and be disbarred," I said.

"Yes, I would have still refused."

Hatfield leaned back in his chair and his eyes searched the ceiling as he recalled his own World War II experience: "I wrote a letter home in 1945 in which I commented that I had seen the utter dregs of colonialism. 'If the West ever thinks it

117

can reimpose its heel on these people, it's totally wrong,' I wrote. 'These people have been spit on long enough, and they've never tolerated Western rule or intervention. There's a nationalism here that will never be put down by Western forces,' I concluded. I had a gift of sensitivity, perhaps," he remarked.

The image I got of Mark Hatfield was one of a man of unbending principle who was unwilling to take the usual routes of compromise and back-room dealings to achieve his political goals. And he had sometimes gotten into trouble with fellow Christians because of his strong beliefs. He had been rejected by a segment of the Evangelical Christian community when he came out strongly against the Vietnam conflict. As a result, he told me, he had been on the verge of not running for a second term as senator in 1972. By speaking against the war and by affirming other traditionally "liberal" causes, he was following a different path from many politically conservative Evangelicals. His position caused him to receive a considerable amount of hate mail and even obscene letters from people who were supposed to be fellow Christians. He felt completely isolated from these Christians. And he was especially moved and actually had to fight back the tears when he was speaking at Fuller Seminary during the war because he saw some supporters put up a banner saying, "We're with you, Mark!" He wasn't sure he wanted to go through this ordeal for another term, but after he won re-election, he came to regard his thoughts of escape as an unacceptable "easy way out."

Lunchtime had arrived, and the Senator invited me to join him and an aide, Vic Glavich, in the Senate dining room. As the three of us stepped onto an elevator, Hatfield gestured toward me and remarked with a grin, "He's a brother."

I was impressed once again with how warm and comforting the Christian fraternity can be. United States senators, world-famous singers, and star athletes can immediately begin to communicate on a deep personal level because of their common allegiance to Christ. When Christ said, "By this all men will know that you are my disciples, if you have love for one another" (John 13:35), He was definitely stating an eternal truth, I thought. His words were as valid in this Senate Office Building, as on the byways of ancient Palestine.

As we sat down to eat, our conversation wandered to mutual acquaintances, and I mentioned that I had recently talked to Pat Boone.

Hatfield said, "Yes, I particularly like the way he signs his letters, 'Another Carpenter's Helper.'"

So Boone's influence reaches even into Christian circles on Capitol Hill, I thought. There seemed to be no escaping the pervasive spiritual impact of the singer, who reminded me more and more of the organizers and leaders of the early New Testament church.

"What about Charles Colson?" I asked. "What do you think about his conversion during the Watergate affair?"

"Chuck and I are in a prayer group together," he said. But he indicated that their relationship hadn't always been so amiable. Mark Hatfield had been one of the people that Colson, as Nixon's special counsel, wanted to discredit during the "dirty tricks" era before the Watergate burglary occurred. The Senator explained that he owned some property which Colson thought might constitute a conflict of interest, so Colson tried to use this information against Hatfield. Even though Colson failed, Hatfield developed an intense dislike for the man. So when former Senator Harold Hughes called Hatfield to tell him about Colson's conversion to Christianity, Hatfield thought it was "a lot of nonsense."

"This guy is for real!" Hughes insisted.

But Hatfield said, "I'll have to see it to believe it."

"Well, Christ converted you, didn't he?" Hughes shot back. "Why shouldn't he convert Colson?"

But Hatfield still wouldn't buy the idea. As he related this story to me, I sensed that this was a case where his high principles might temporarily have taken precedence over establishing a personal relationship. But then Hatfield was invited by his old friend and former student, Doug Coe, to a small prayer session with six other men before a Presidential Prayer Breakfast. Hatfield accepted and when he walked into the room he saw several familiar, friendly faces—evangelist Billy Graham, Congressman Al Quie, Graham Purcell, Senator Harold Hughes, and Coe. But the only empty seat was next to a not-so-friendly face—his old enemy, Charles Colson.

"My first impulse was to turn around and walk out," Hatfield recalled.

He finally decided to take the seat, and the group began to share with one another and finally dropped to their knees to pray. Hatfield was the last to offer a prayer, and he recalled, "Something prompted me to pray for Chuck Colson, and also to pray for forgiveness for the attitude I held toward him."

When they finished praying and stood up, the two old enemies, Hatfield and Colson, embraced. Hatfield now refers to Colson with the same words he used to describe me in the elevator: "He's a brother."

I had been bothered by some of the same suspicions that Senator Hatfield harbored when I had traveled to Washington on an earlier occasion to visit with Colson himself. We had arranged to meet at Fellowship House in an exclusive section of the city near the Shoreham Hotel. As I sipped coffee on expensive china and waited for him in an elegantly furnished drawing room, I thought cynically, "It's not so bad, being a Christian in these surroundings."

The only things I knew about Colson were what I had read in articles or heard him say on television. His book, *Born Again,* had not been published at the time. I wanted to believe his spiritual commitment was genuine, mainly because I can't stand people who use their Christianity to accomplish some ulterior motive, such as getting public sympathy. Colson had already served his jail term for attempted obstruction of justice in the Daniel Ellsberg "Pentagon Papers" case. Since his license to practice law was in jeopardy, I couldn't help wondering whether he was looking for a lucrative new career in religion.

Although I had seen many pictures of Colson—heard him described as "owl-like" and tough as nails—I almost didn't recognize him as he strode across the room to greet me. He was much larger—well over six feet—and friendlier and warmer than I had expected. Somehow, it was hard to believe this guy had been former President Nixon's "hatchet man."

As we began to talk, I could detect the intensity and single-mindedness that had catapulted him into a $100,000-a-year law practive and also into one of the most powerful positions in national government as Nixon's special counsel. His schedule

120

was apparently as packed as it had ever been in the White House. He had just been interviewed by a CBS television reporter, and he would be going to another engagement that evening when we had completed our talk. A few strands of his neatly parted hair hung down across his forehead and he smoked one cigarette after another. "There are lots of problems I face as a Christian, but one of the toughest is living up to the kind of standard I think I should live up to," he said. "Like this cigarette. I can't quit smoking. I'm weak. I'll quit and then go back. It's terrible."

Chuck Colson didn't strike me as the kind of guy who was just trying to make a good impression. He was simply trying to be honest by showing not only the progress he had made since his conversion, but also his failures and shortcomings. The more he talked, the more convinced I became that my original skepticism about his commitment to Christ was unfounded.

Knowing that a conversation with Tom Phillips, President of the Raytheon Corporation, in Massachusetts, had been decisive in his conversion, I asked, "Would you say your commitment was the result of some search for the meaning of life?"

"I had no spiritual longings," he said bluntly. "I had a dead feeling, but I wasn't searching for anything spiritual. There was no consciousness of sin, of separation from God. But I remember as Nixon, Bob Haldeman, and I sat around the Oval Office on election night [1972], I felt this tremendous sense of emptiness instead of elation that we had just won this historic election."

"The decisive thing was Phillips, right?"

"That March encounter [in 1973] with Phillips was the most amazing thing in my life," Chuck replied. "It's one reason I feel led now to give my time and life to evangelism, to spreading the Good News. Before Phillips, no one ever came up to me and said, 'Have you thought about whether you could have a personal relationship with God?' I would have said, 'No, I never thought about it.' Maybe I could have been led to Christ. It's amazing, but no one ever asked that. One of my oldest friends, who has known Christ for years, never discussed it with me."

His observation impressed me, and I began to think back over the many people with whom I had failed to share my faith.

121

It was a disturbing idea—that hundreds of people like Colson may have passed through my life, and I had lost opportunities to tell them about my relationship with God. "Why do you think Phillips decided to talk with you?" I wondered.

"He was following the Scriptural admonitions to be bold in your faith," Colson declared. "Of course, I raised the issue. I said, 'Something has happened to you, you've changed.' He said, 'I've accepted Jesus Christ and committed my life to Him.' There was a peaceful radiance about him that showed he cared about me. He and I were much alike. We were sons of immigrant parents, went through school at night, fought our way to the top. At first, he put me off. I thought he was some kind of nut. But his words made me curious. Then, when he prayed, he sounded like he was talking to God. That was the first time I'd ever heard that. That sent me into orbit—that you could pray and God might really hear you. Here was a guy who was educated, articulate, an industrious businessman. And he wasn't ashamed to pray out loud. That made an impact on me."

"Do you think your conversion, your willingness to listen to Phillips, resulted from the Watergate affair?" I asked, wondering if a "foxhole religion" mentality had driven him to God because of the possibility of a career disaster in his life.

"I didn't consider myself even remotely involved then," he said. "In the spring of '73, Watergate was building, but I thought I was in the clear. My conversion wasn't brought about by Watergate, but Watergate helped. It wasn't that I thought I'd be a criminal defendant, but rather, the feeling that all the values I had in life were being turned upside down. There was fear too—fear of seeing your whole career topple down with Watergate. I was concerned that my name was being blackened every day in the headlines in the Washington *Post*. My law career, my reputation as a lawyer, the ability to attract clients, would suffer. I wondered whether my whole career would be wrecked."

For a week after his second meeting with Phillips, Colson studied and meditated in a cottage on the Maine coast. Then he made his decision. "It didn't take more than a minute," he told me. "I sat down and prayed by myself: 'I ask you to come into my life, be my Lord; I want you in my life, Lord Jesus.' There

122

was no sense of urgency. It was just a decision I had come to, an act of the will. That's the way I believe it is with everybody. I felt released, freed, happy, excited. It was as though I was letting out a big sigh. I had found out what life was all about. Watergate, what happened to my friend the President, my law practice—all these things began to seem much less important. I got an eternal perspective.

"As we drove back to Boston the next day, I felt so much better. Usually on my first day back in Washington after a trip, I was the busy lawyer and government executive. You go right past crowds and know they're looking at you because you're the public personality. You don't see them individually. As I rushed from limousine to limousine, I'd just see a blur. But that day I remember seeing every individual. My conversion slowed me down. I saw the whole world didn't revolve around me. There were lots of 'me's.' Every other individual was as important as I was. Christianity is a great leveler. The world revolves around God, I realized."

Although Chuck had once prided himself on being tough and calculating, his emotions did an about-face. "I was a guy who had believed in the *macho* syndrome—all toughness," he said. "But I was crying so hard after I left Tom Phillips [on the second visit] that I couldn't drive the car away. I'd never cried before like that. Now, sometimes I'll start crying when I pray— just burst into tears—and I'm not a tearful kind of person. Sometimes I'll be speaking and feel the tears well up and have to fight them, but in a small group, it doesn't bother me. We [the members of his prayer group] often have tears during prayer."

He has also had some experiences with the Holy Spirit which have altered all his former notions of rational conduct. "In prison I was feeling low during a Bible study on the indwelling of the Holy Spirit. The teacher explained you just have to ask for that experience to get it, so I started praying. I felt an unmistakable physical sensation bubbling over. It continued for quite a while—an effervescent, tingling sensation. I was very excited about it." His description reminded me of Graham Kerr's references to a "spiritual sparklet" feeling during his conversion. "It was a tremendous surging feeling, as though the Spirit was moving through my body," Colson told me. "I prayed

123

again and had the same experience again. It affected the way I related to the people around me. It was almost like renewing the conversion experience. Then I prayed with a Baptist preacher, and felt the Holy Spirit knock me on my knees. It came out of left field."

But the day I spoke with him, I sensed that the initial euphoria of Colson's commitment had departed and that he seemed slightly harried and weighed down by the responsibilities thrust upon him as a famous new Christian. "I have days now when I feel burned out, not worthy," he confided. "I feel like I'm going to quit and not do anything. It's the typical downs. I was at a tremendous city-wide rally where there was a tremendous response in decisions for Christ. I was there with my head down, and I wondered, 'Am I on an ego trip? Why am I doing this?' But you have days like that."

"You get paid for these appearances, don't you?" I asked.

"Yes, but all my speaking fees I donate to Fellowship House," he replied.

"You seem quite busy—even rushed and a little harried," I observed.

"Christianity isn't all an easy way. People think it's a cop-out in times of trouble. Kids think they'll get better grades in school if they pray. But I've found you bear other people's burdens like your own. It's no easy way. You suffer with other people. I was in here at seven this morning, and I'll be leaving at seven tonight. I'm every bit as tired as I was in the White House, solving what I thought were world-shaking problems.

"There's a frustration in not being able to do enough. I've had that all my life, in everything I've ever done. And I have it now in the cause of Christ, I have a calendar that won't quit. Some brother is always asking me to go to a prayer breakfast in his city. But every day I'm away is a day I'm not with my family. It's not an easy life. It's a hard life of self-denial."

I knew these weren't just empty words that he was handing me. He was already in the process of starting a nationwide prison ministry which would involve networks of prayer fellowships among inmates. The demands on him as a speaker were escalating. And though he said his wife, Patty, was behind him, he still faced skepticism from other members of his family: "My older son thought I was a Jesus freak and probably still does. My mother was horrified. She called her friends and said, 'Imagine, my boy saying he wasn't a Christian before! We brought him up in a fine home. We took him to Sunday school.' It was toughest in my own family. It's harder to talk to my own children about Christ than to large audiences." His problem reminded me of the difficulties Jesus predicted many believers would face in relating to their family members (Luke 12:49–53).

Chuck also still experiences rejection from his old friends. "I feel repudiated by them because they say, 'We like the way you were.' These are people who used to work with me, and they take it as a repudiation of themselves. The scoffing doesn't bother me, though. I would have been a scoffer myself under similar circumstances. I can understand cynical people. Sometimes the Lord uses that attitude, because it can make them curious. Whenever a secular press guy says, 'Are you for real?' I say, 'You have to judge for yourself.' That's opening that guy up, challenging him."

Chuck still bemoaned the fact that he had lost opportunities to discuss his faith with Richard Nixon. "I don't feel I've effectively witnessed to him, and I was a guy who had a real opportunity to do so," he said. "I believe I failed him. Now I don't talk to him regularly, but once in a while. We have a cordial relationship."

After we had talked for more than an hour, Chuck told me he had to be leaving for his next appointment. But as I started to get my things together to leave, he stopped me.

"Let's not go without a minute's prayer," he said.

"Okay."

We sat down at a table and bowed our heads, and he prayed. "Father, we thank you for the time you've given us together and I would just ask you to be with Bill now as he writes and as he continues his walk with you. We thank you, Lord, that we can know what it is to be in fellowship, even in these few brief moments, when it seems like the pressures of the day crowd in on us. But we thank you above all that you've called us to these things. I ask that you'll be with Bill now as he travels back to New York. Just protect him, Lord. Use him and speak through him to reach others. Help us to be better servants. In the name of Jesus Christ we pray. Amen."

Then I said, "Lord, I thank you for this opportunity to meet Chuck here, and I pray you'll be with him as he goes along with his frenetic schedule. Give him a sense of calmness and peace as he trusts in you and provides this much-needed Christian leadership. In Jesus' name. Amen."

"Umm, thanks," he murmured.

Colson dropped me off at the Shoreham Hotel where I could get a taxi to the Washington train station. As I watched him accelerate down the highway toward his next appointment, I couldn't help but remember something he had told me about his preferences in music. As a former hard-charging Marine company commander, and tough White House aide, his favorite song had been "The Marine Hymn," and he had marched most of his life to this aggressive, *macho* beat.

"I don't really know what my favorite is now," he told me with a grin, "but I do like 'Onward, Christian Soldiers.'"

## Chapter 9

# *Jimmy's Little Sister*
# *Meets the Press*
## RUTH CARTER STAPLETON

"Mrs. Stapleton, I have one more question about your brother," a tough New York female reporter said. "He keeps talking about being a 'born-again Christian, bathed in the blood of the Lamb.' As a non-Christian, I'd like to know what precisely does that mean in political terms?"

Ruth Carter Stapleton—evangelist, healer, and sister of Jimmy Carter—sighed. In an effort to promote her book, *The Gift of Inner Healing,* she was meeting the New York press in a conference room above the Logos Bookstore near Grand Central Station. It was April 1976, in the middle of the presidential primaries. The questions from the scores of newspaper and television reporters were coming hard and fast—especially from a couple of female journalists who stood only a few feet from her.

"This is oversimplistic," Ruth answered, "but we are body, mind, and spirit. Many people go through life being aware only of our body and mind. A spiritual awakening involves coming into that dimension of understanding and awareness that you're a spiritual being. It's like a birth process, but it's a complete awareness."

"What does that mean to the nation politically?" the woman

127

pressed, and several guffaws and titters erupted around the room.

"It means this [the born-again politician] will be a man who will have emotional stability and peace," Ruth replied.

The toughest questions continued to come from the female members of the press, who seemed determined to prove that religion and politics don't mix. Here are a few typical exchanges:

Reporter: "Some people say he [Jimmy Carter] likes to keep the fact that he has a sister who is an evangelist a secret—is this true or not?"

Ruth (defiantly): "I don't think so. In several interviews he's had, he didn't seem to want to keep it a secret. I think he's proud of me."

Reporter: "Right. You've said in one interview this could be the first time in our country's history we've had a President who has made a public commitment to Christ. Can you explain the significance of this?"

Ruth: "I didn't make an absolute statement like that."

Reporter: "It was in the Washington *Star*. Do you take it back?"

Ruth: "No, I . . . I don't think he would be the first President . . . I don't know that much about the backgrounds of the different Presidents."

Reporter: "All right, is it important [for presidential candidates] to make a public commitment to Christ?"

Ruth: "Let me put it this way: I think it's the most important thing in the world that we have a President who is committed to truth and honesty and integrity and to the principles and teachings of Christ. If he were not a Christian and were committed to the teachings of Christ which I have just named, I think that would be good too. But honesty and integrity to me are so important. I happen to be a Christian, and I believe Christ is the way, so therefore I'm very committed in that way. But I do believe we do need a strong leader."

Reporter: "I'd like to clear up something. When you speak about the teachings of Christ, do you mean truth, honesty, and integrity, or do you mean something more?"

Ruth (apparently getting somewhat frustrated): "This really gets into almost a religious discussion. Is that what you want?"

128

Reporter: "Well now, I'm leading up to the fact that religion and politics mix in his book and in yours. I'm asking you, *do* religion and politics mix? Here you are promoting a book . . ."

Ruth: "I think religion and politics mix. Religion and housewife duties, religion and everything mix. What is religion? It is being dedicated to the highest and the best, committing all you are to a way of life that uses the highest potential of your integrity. What we often think about is the hypocrisy—using religion as a tool to gain something. It's one thing just to go to church on Sunday, but it's a different story to live a life twenty-four hours a day, committed to the highest you can be."

Reporter: "So if it's not a Christian ethic, but an ethic devoted to the highest in you, that would be all right?"

Ruth: "To me it would, but I'm not putting words in anybody's mouth—especially not Jimmy's."

As I listened to this heated dialogue, I was fascinated by what a strange happening I was witnessing. Who would ever have imagined, even a year before, that the faith-healing sister of an Evangelical Christian presidential candidate would be undergoing such a grilling under glaring TV lights by the cynical New York press corps? It was almost surrealistic, more like the fantasy of a sensationalistic Hollywood scriptwriter than a real event.

Blond, bouncy Ruth seemed much younger than her forty-six years, and she was doing a good job fending off the attacks and fielding the pointed queries. But it must have been disconcerting for her to hear hard news reporters asking about the political implications of being "born again" and "bathed in the blood of the Lamb." Identifying with Ruth's struggle to convey her message to the hostile listeners, I watched the verbal battle with much the same anticipation that I might view a suspense movie —to see whether the heroine would come out on top.

The inquisition continued:

Reporter: "Jimmy has said he never lied. Did he ever tell just a little white lie?"

Ruth: "He never said he never lied. He just said he will not lie to you or deceive you. He won't hide the truth from you."

Reporter: "Did he ever tell a *little* white lie?"

Ruth (sighing): "My mother [Lillian] called the other day and said, 'For goodness sakes, please try to help me think of something bad Jimmy did for these reporters!' I thought and thought of two or three things that Jimmy did that were bad."

Reporter: "What were they?"

Ruth: "I'm sure you'll be reading them in the paper. It's so ridiculous. When my little brother Billy was two years old, we all dressed to go to Sunday School in our best clothes. Jimmy picked Billy up and said, 'If you don't say uncle, I'm going to pour this bottle of hair oil in your mouth!' Billy kept holding his mouth shut, and Jimmy squeezed him until he opened his mouth. The top came off, and Billy's mouth was filled with it and his clothes were ruined. He [Jimmy] got a terrible whipping for that."

Reporter (writing furiously): "How old was Jimmy then?"

Ruth: "Let's see . . . Billy was two, and Jimmy was five years older than me, and I'm eight years older than Billy. You'll have to figure it out."

Reporter: "How much money did Behold Inc. [Ruth's evangelistic organization] make last year?"

Ruth: "We came out even, no profit. When it doesn't come out even, my husband supplements. He's a veterinarian. We used up all our savings . . ."

Reporter: "Do you use Jesus in all of your imagery?"

Ruth: "Yes, even when I'm with secular groups."

Reporter: "Are your work and your spiritual contacts helping your brother politically?"

Ruth: "Up to this point, it's been a detriment."

Reporter: "A detriment?"

Ruth: "That's one of those misquotes."

Reporter: "You made it."

Ruth (somewhat disconcerted): "I know it . . . I'm amazed at the questions I've gotten . . ."

Reporter: "I'm asking if your contacts are helping Jimmy."

Ruth: "I think people are beginning to put two and two together. But many times people don't know I'm Jimmy's sister. No one approached me in Houston with a group of a thousand —no one there knew I was Jimmy's sister. I'm not introduced as Jimmy Carter's sister."

Her smile was looking somewhat strained, but the creamy Southern accent, combined with her attempts to be honest and forthright, seemed to be winning the reporters to her side. Or perhaps they were just getting tired of the intensity of the encounter. In any case, the questions, rather than being so argumentative, seemed to become more interested and exploratory.

Reporter: "Do you object to the name 'faith healer'?"

Ruth: "I've never heard of myself or thought of myself that way. Everybody has different connotations for words. To me, 'faith healer' signifies a person having a gift no one else has. This is not the way I feel at all. I feel the only gift I have is a commitment of my life to serve. I think any other committed person to a high cause would be able to do the same things I do."

Reporter: "Have you ever been able to heal anyone physically?"

Ruth: "Oh, consantly. You see, the ministry is in three parts —prayer for physical, emotional, and spiritual healing."

Reporter: "What kind of physical illnesses have you cured?"

Ruth: "I haven't cured any, but I've been the catalyst for the Spirit to work through me. I'm not a faith healer, but a catalyst for God, if you want to put it that way. God is the healer. I've had . . . well, you may not believe it, but I've seen the blind from birth healed. I've actually prayed and seen the creative energy flow from a body where a lame child walked for the first time. In Indonesia, three deaf-mutes came, and before the week ended, all three deaf-mutes were completely healed. I haven't seen as many traumatic, dramatic healings in the United States as in other countries. But I've seen a few in the last year. A child, the son of a doctor, had undergone five heart operations and had one side withered. After an experience of prayer with a team of three, and undergirding support from another [prayer] group, that child was completely healed—length of arms, width of shoulders, everything."

Reporter: "What part did you play in these healings?"

Ruth: "I think that, because my faith has been growing for the last sixteen years, my faith may be contagious to those with less faith. My ministry is to help that person to have faith in a higher power, in Christ. It's a process that works in their hearts."

Reporter: "Do you think maybe Jimmy's political campaign is some divine plan to bring attention to your work?"

131

Ruth (laughing): "I don't know. I had as much work as I could handle before Jimmy announced."

Reporter: "Can you tell us about Jimmy's religious experience?"

Ruth: "Well, it was just a part of a series of different experiences that Jimmy had. It didn't seem so mammoth until just the last few weeks. Then everybody has said, 'What happened under the pine trees?' But it was a sharing we had. Jimmy and I worked together in the campaign, when he ran against Lester Mattox. Jimmy had known me only as a spoiled brat, selfish and demanding. I don't know what changes he saw, but he saw some changes and simply asked me if we could talk. So a brother and sister got away from the rest of the family, to sit and talk alone. What Jimmy wanted to know was what Christ really meant to me.

"So I shared with Jimmy my experience, how I moved in my relationship from an intellectual understanding of a historical figure who lived two thousand years ago, to an awareness of a personal relationship with a person who lives now, the same as yesterday. As I shared my experience, I think Jimmy was probably relating it to his own experience. You know, spiritual growth is not a one-time thing. It's a process. This was a part of the process. So I shared what it meant to me—to come to a place of real, total commitment. When I was ready to give up everything for Christ, [I found] the peace, the joy, and the power that it brings. [During] most of this, I remember Jimmy said, 'Yes, I understand.' He didn't share with me a lot of what went on in his mind. I was coming from an intuitive, emotional experience, and Jimmy was relating it to his reasonable, logical mind. We're two different minds."

As the first part of the press conference drew to a close, someone announced that in a few minutes Mrs. Stapleton would be conducting a "directed daydream" session to illustrate her methods of spiritual group psychotherapy. Although anyone who wanted to participate was invited to stay, I think the assumption was that most of the reporters would leave. But as far as I could tell, no one even looked toward the exit. During the break, I walked over to Ruth with the intention of clearing up a few questions I had about her religious background. She had seemed to play down the exact nature of her spiritual renewal experience. I suspected the reason for her reticence might have had something to do with the fact that she was a Southern Baptist who had become involved in the Charismatic Renewal Movement. Some Southern Baptist churches have condemned the Charismatic Movement—with its stress on tongues, prophecies, and healings—as being non-Scriptural, unauthentic Christianity, and I suspected Ruth might want to avoid any public conflict on this issue.

"Are you a member of the Charismatic Movement yourself?" I asked her.

"There's no membership," she replied. "There are some charismatics I would identify with, others I wouldn't identify with. As far as those who say you've got to speak in tongues, I don't identify with that at all."

"You don't speak in tongues?"

"Yes, but I don't adopt the belief that you've got to speak in tongues," she said. "The Charismatic Movement means a renewal of spirit and power."

"Do you regard your experience at that retreat, where you had sort of a turn around spiritually, as a renewal or conversion?" I asked.

"I think it was a real breakthrough," she said cagily. Some of her brother's political skills had definitely rubbed off on her.

"Do you consider yourself to have been a Christian before that experience?" I asked, trying to get at the answer another way.

"Yes, as far as the fundamental terms of being saved for eternal life, I'd consider that I had been saved for eternal life. But that [the renewal] brought me into an awareness of learning to live the life here on this earth. I never think about life after death. I'm not even interested in life after death. It's all helping people to learn to cope with life here."

"So your renewal was a sort of a 'baptism of the Spirit' experience?"

"Yes," she said.

By this time, other reporters had started moving in our direction, but most of them had crowded behind Ruth where I could see them and she couldn't. Before someone else cornered her, I decided to probe her personal feelings and reactions to the press ordeal she had just faced. "What's your feeling right now? I mean, do you feel under pressure now?" I asked. "Those were some pretty tough questions that you were asked."

She glanced behind her, saw the other reporters, and immediately tightened up. The public façade that seemed to have been slipping slightly in our conversation was now firmly back in place. She answered hurriedly, "Oh, no. Uh, uh. Because I don't mind saying I don't know. I don't have to be political. I'm not a political person."

Then she told me she had to get ready for the next part of her presentation and walked quickly toward Roger Kenworthy, the Logos bookstore executive who had organized the event. I got the impression that, regardless of how well she could handle herself with the press, she wished she could escape for a few moments from the penetrating eyes of public scrutiny and talk openly with some friend about her frustrations and faith, without any fear of news media repercussions.

At the beginning of the second part of the press conference, Ruth explained some of her techniques of "inner healing," or spiritual psychotherapy. "There are five basic negatives, which cause most of our problems," she began. "Those are fear, frustration, inferiority, guilt, and loneliness. You have to be as a little child—put your mind up on a shelf—for inner healing. Perfect, universal love, the healing agent, has to bypass consciousness. Inner healing is communicating love to the negative, repressed aspects of the human being. My theory is that from the time of conception, maybe the fourth month in the womb, a child can pick up negative emotions from the surrounding atmosphere. This makes it possible for a child to come into the world already damaged. So we have to bypass the mind. All of us are walking around with some repressed negatives within us, and most of these negatives occur from the time of conception to the age of five years."

Then she said she was going to demonstrate her technique through a "directed daydream," but she hesitated. All the tough reporters, who had been attacking her earlier, were still sitting out there. I could imagine she didn't see this as a particularly receptive audience for spiritual group therapy.

She cleared her throat and said, "If you wouldn't like to participate and want to leave, I'd like you to leave now. I wouldn't want anybody to be a captive audience. I know you might have a luncheon appointment." She hesitated, apparently hoping that the majority of her listeners would file out. But nobody budged, so she continued: "I'm going to skip to the period when you were five years old," she began. "Close your eyes if you want to participate." But as she looked around, most people still stared at her with wide-open eyes. "If you want to write, it's okay," she said tentatively. "But just to hear it intellectually won't mean anything. It has to be experienced to be understood."

Then she plunged into the therapy session: "I always begin on a cushion of perfect love. As unconditional love touches you and the Spirit begins to move, a lot of times, even out of a group of a thousand, what's repressed comes up to consciousness. I'll have at least three women who have been molested, [been the objects of] incest by their fathers. This will bring out a tremendous shrill or scream because it's been repressed."

I had half-closed my eyes, but at her statement I furtively glanced around to see if there were any such reactions in our group. I noticed several other reporters had their pencils poised too, in case there were any emotional outbreaks worth recording.

"We begin by enveloping that person in perfect love," she repeated. "Jesus is the only one who gave perfect, unconditional love. Even though I'm a Protestant, I think the mother Mary gave perfect mother love to Jesus. He received perfect love and was not scarred as a child. As we close our eyes, I affirm that perfect love is moving around and about and within each one of us. As you breathe, you breathe in the Holy Spirit, that Christ Spirit, that perfect love that brings peace and love."

I was getting more into the mood now, but I couldn't help reflecting again how incredible it was that the sister of a U.S. presidential candidate was actually pulling something like this off with a bunch of hard-nosed New York City reporters. As I looked around, many more people had closed their eyes and

135

everyone was deadly serious and completely quiet. The noisy press conference had almost been transformed into a church sanctuary.

"As you breathe"—there was a loud rush of air in the room —"allow that warmth in. Use your imaginations. Maybe there's a golden light flowing through your body, or a stream of cool water. Water is imagery for the spiritual life. Now, in your imagination, visualize yourself at age five. Think of the house where you lived. Think of a room in that house where you felt real comfortable. See yourself sitting on the bed, or chair, or sofa, and Jesus walks into the room. Jesus is the epitome of perfect love as He puts His arm around you. He knows everything about you, knows all your hurts, every fear you ever experienced, all the little feelings of inferiority. And He loves you with perfect love. Rest in Him. And by faith, I claim as you sit there, with Jesus' arms around you, that the negative is being drawn out of you and consumed in that perfect love that He has for you. Every negative feeling, every negative emotion, every bit of guilt."

By now, I was completely into the fantasy world she had created, but I felt obligated to jerk myself back to reality periodically just so I wouldn't miss anything that was going on. I suspected other reporters in the room were having similar inner struggles. "Now, as you sit there in His love," she said, "I want you to imagine that your mother walks into the room and comes face to face with you. And as you look into her eyes, look deeper than you can see physically. I want you to look into your mother's entire life. And as you look, you'll see she's had hurts and pains you never knew about—desires that were unfulfilled.

"As you're bathed in that unconditional love of Jesus within your heart, think these thoughts: 'Mother, I do know that you were the best mother you could be under the circumstances of your life. And I forgive you of all the love I needed that you weren't able to give.' Now, in your imagination, take by faith that Spirit of perfect love in Jesus. That love flows through Him as He reaches out and symbolically touches you, and as He touches your mother. I claim that every barrier is melted between the two of you. You can be united in a perfect, healed relationship. He bridges that gap between that love you needed,

136

and that love you got. And I ask that there will be a sense of peace in this united relationship—the perfect child-mother relationship."

I looked up and . . . was it possible that one of those tough female reporters was brushing a tear away from her eye? Surely not, I thought, but after all, I had been getting a little choked up myself.

"Now you see your mother walk out of the room," Ruth said. "Now we bring your father in. Sense your daddy coming in. He comes over to you, sits down in front of you, and you look into his eyes. Look deeply. Maybe you had him on a pedestal. You expected more of him than a human being could ever be. Maybe you didn't realize he was human, fallible with weaknesses, longings, and a lot of hurt that was unhealed."

I was having trouble fighting back the tears now. Afraid to look up for fear one of the other press people would see my eyes glistening, I fiddled in a businesslike way with my tape recorder.

"Maybe he wanted to take you in his arms, but he couldn't," Ruth said. "As you recognized him as a person, a human being for the first time, you say, 'I give you freedom to fail, Dad. I give you freedom to make mistakes in my life. I know you were the best daddy you could be under the circumstances of your background, your childhood, your environment.' Now say to him, 'Dad, forgive me of all the pain I ever caused you.' As Jesus blesses you and your father, we thank you, Jesus, that this child-father relationship is made whole in You. Finally, in your imagination, see your father move out of the room.

"Now move up to the present time. Know that every relationship you have has been colored by the relationship you had with your mother and father. Know that this is a process that must continue as the deepest levels of the negatives in your life are touched by His love. We thank you, Jesus, that these relationships have been made whole in perfect love through you. Amen."

There was a lengthy silence after she had finished, and finally the audience of journalists began to stir and move about. I heard one of the reporters say to a companion, "This is the first time I've ever seen a group of reporters this quiet."

I had to agree. Several of the newspaper and television people, who had seemed the most hostile at first, now were all smiles and engaged in intimate conversations with Ruth. Their articles the next day were uniformly positive. Jimmy's little sister had apparently won the hearts of the New York City press corps.

# Chapter 10

# *A Cure for Moon Sickness*
## ASTRONAUT JAMES IRWIN

Wearing his bulky white spacesuit, Colonel Jim Irwin, the Apollo 15 astronaut, was stretched out flat on his back at my feet. He was in the middle of taping a television program for an independent Christian producer in Philadelphia, and the weight of the hot, sixty-pound suit, combined with delays in the rehearsal schedule, had finally compelled him to lie down exhausted on the stage.

As I knelt beside him to ask a few questions during the break, a wave of nausea rolled over me, and I realized I was actually in worse shape than Irwin. When I had awakened in our apartment in New York earlier that morning, I had a feeling I should call and cancel the interview because I was feeling queasier than normal before breakfast. But I had been having so much trouble pinning the astronaut down for a talk that I decided I'd better try to go through with it. Because Irwin travels throughout the world on speaking engagements for his High Flight evangelistic organization, I knew he might be thousands of miles away if I tried to reach him on another date.

Unfortunately, my worst fears were realized when I got sick on the train to Philadelphia. I was still feeling very weak because I couldn't keep any food in my stomach. Trying to push my own discomfort out of my mind, I looked down at his sharp-featured face, with that prominent moon-shaped scar on his chin, and commented, "You look a little tired, Jim."

139

"Yeah, this thing is hot and heavy," he said, gesturing at the outsized spacesuit. His bare head, protruding out the top, seemed small and incongruous in comparison to the outfit.

"You were a Christian when you went to the moon?" I asked.

"Yes, I asked Jesus into my life when I was eleven years old," he replied in the clipped tones of a high-ranking Air Force officer. He wasted no words and got right to the point. All business.

"But you had your spiritual ups and downs, didn't you?"

"True," he said thoughtfully. "I had that conversion experience when I was eleven, but I drifted in and out of churches for several years. Shortly before the moon flight [in 1971], I decided to take my kids to Sunday School because I felt it was important for a child's upbringing. But I was never active in the church. I sat there as a kind of 'bump-on-a-log' Christian. Very passive. Or, as [TV evangelist] Rex Humbard would say, kind of a mannequin."

"But when you went up in space on the Apollo 15 flight, did you sense God up there?"

"Right," he replied. "A spiritual awakening occurred because of the things I saw and felt. What really impressed me was to see the earth as just a beautiful jewel in the sky. To see the earth with the eyes of God, and realize it's a precious place, probably the only home for men. Seeing it shrink in size allowed me to realize how small I was physically, and in a spiritual way to see things in God's universe that very few have had the opportunity to see. I was amazed while traveling through God's universe."

The astronaut then glanced around with an annoyed look and began to express some of the building impatience he was feeling as a result of the rehearsal delays. "Let us know when they're ready to shoot!" he called out to one of the producers. "I'm just lying by."

I smiled at the reference to his horizontal position. But my nausea squelched my amusement and I quickly excused myself and headed toward the restroom. I hadn't mentioned my virus, or whatever it was, to Jim because it somehow seemed unprofessional and maybe even potentially frightening to tell an interviewee that I wasn't feeling well and might vomit in his face at any moment. I suppose I also didn't want to put his Christian love to too severe a test by confronting him with a possibly infectious flu germ—especially since he had told me he was just recovering from a bug himself. I tried drinking a lukewarm Coke before I returned to the stage, but that sent me back to the restroom again. I could see it was definitely going to be a bad day.

Irwin was standing up talking to one of the TV people when I finally returned, and I could hear him reprimanding the man for the delays in the production schedule. "I think the Lord expects us to do as good and efficient a job for Christ as secular television people do for their bosses," he was saying. My fears deepened that he would be even more impatient with me if he knew I was exposing him to a virus. And the more I thought about it, the more I realized how silly and irresponsible I'd been to try to go through with the interview. I couldn't help but recall the Golden Rule that Jesus had stressed as a basic guide for Christian conduct: ". . . as you wish that men would do to you, do so to them" (Luke 6:31; Matthew 7:12). I certainly would not have wanted Jim Irwin to expose me to the flu, and so I could see how wrong I was in putting him in a similar danger.

Irwin's obvious emphasis on excellence and responsible action indicated to me that it wasn't just by chance that he had worked his way up to the top of the nation's Air Force establishment and qualified as an astronaut. But the story he began to relate on camera—like the one he had told me in private—showed that he felt God deserved most of the credit for his achievements.

"I'm grateful to God that he allowed me to go to the moon, but I'm much more grateful that He brought me back to earth so that I could be here as part of this program," he said as the TV cameras started to hover around him. "That flight really changed my life. God touched my life, but it wasn't the first time."

He went on to explain how his mother and father had guided him toward God until he accepted Christ during a church service in Florida at the age of eleven. At an invitation from a pastor during an altar call, he said, "I simply stood up with a few other young people and moved forward. Tears were streaming down my face at such a happy moment, just inviting Jesus Christ into my life to be my Lord and Savior, cementing a relationship I've needed every day of my life. Little did I realize how much I would need the Lord or just where I would need Him."

He eventually went to the U. S. Naval Academy, switched to the Air Force and finally became a test pilot. "How proud I was," he recalled. "I really thought I was the hottest pilot in the sky. I was on cloud nine, and should have known I was in for a letdown."

He went out flying one morning in a small plane with a student pilot who was at the controls, and the aircraft went into an uncontrollable spin and crashed. Both men were severely injured, and Irwin suffered two broken legs, a broken jaw, and many cuts and bruises.

When he finally woke up in the hospital, he said to himself, "Could this really have happened to me, to Jim Irwin, the hottest pilot in the sky?" He recalled it was a "humbling feeling, to bite the dust in such an inglorious way. My next thought was just a question: 'Lord, why did You let this happen to me? Why raise me up to the very heights and let me fall so low? Why did You let this happen?' I prayed to God harder than I ever had before, asking for understanding. And God answered those prayers. I quickly realized I had been rushing through life too fast, not fully appreciating the daily plusses of life. God also answered my prayers for recovery."

His wounds finally healed and he was able to return to his job as test pilot. And in 1966 he was selected as a member of the U.S. astronaut team. After five years of training and preparation, Jim became a part of the Apollo 15 moon flight with Al Worden and Dave Scott. The blast-off was scheduled for July 26, 1971, "A day I'll never forget, a day that began very early," he recalled. The first words he heard at 4:30 A.M. that day were from Deke Slayton, his "boss" at NASA: "Okay, guys, you ready to go to the moon today?" Deke asked.

"We had a big breakfast, and then into this suit," he said, pointing to the huge white spacesuit. "There were no clouds in the sky. It was a joy to be alive. We didn't talk very much, so many thoughts were racing through our minds. We saw the spacecraft, towering up above us, and what a beautiful sight it was!"

Then it was up the elevators to the top of the rocket and into the spacecraft. "They closed that big steel hatch, bang! like a dungeon door. We realized this was no longer a practice or dry run. That was a moment of truth. They were really sending us to the moon. That gets you right down here, in the pit of your stomach."

The last minutes went extremely fast. "Before we knew it, we heard the word 'ignition,'" he said. "Then we felt and heard all that tremendous power underneath that rocket, beginning to lift us off the earth. It was a moment of extreme elation, almost the happiest moment of my life. A complete release of tension. After all these years of preparation and training, at last it was my turn, at last I was leaving the earth. Most importantly, we knew we had the prayers of men and women, boys and girls on the earth.

"We had a beautiful flight, and we saw things we would never see again in our mortal lives. The most magnificent sight was that first view we had of the earth. We could see it as just a ball in the heavens. We were out about fifty thousand miles, and we were maneuvering the spacecraft when the earth drifted into the center of my window. I looked out and I just couldn't believe my eyes. Such a magnificent sight! So I called to Dave and Al, and I said, 'Guys, come over here and look at this!' Very quickly, the two of them floated over to the window, and there it was. You could see the warm, natural colors, the tans of the deserts, the blues and greens of the oceans, and the white of the clouds. We were reminded of a Christmas tree ornament hanging there in the blackness of space."

I thought how appropriate the image was since it was now only a few days before Christmas. His description was so vivid and fascinating that I had almost forgotten I was sick.

"It seemed like the most delicate, the most fragile Christmas tree ornament you could ever imagine," Jim continued. "It looked as if we could somehow reach out and touch it with our fingers and the whole thing would just crumble, fall apart."

He also told the TV audience, as he had mentioned to me earlier, that one of the most deeply moving things he noticed was how the earth shrank in size as the spacecraft sped farther away. "From the size of a basketball, to the size of a baseball, to the size of a golf ball, to the size of a marble," he said. "You looked back and realized everything you ever cared about and loved was out there. That does something to you inside. It brings a man back profoundly changed, with a deep appreciation for the earth and everything we have on it. We were very privileged, and from that trip I have a new sense of God's creation, His control, and His closeness."

Jim continued to feel God's presence even when he was on the moon. The Lunar Module landed at a prepicked campsite at the base of the Apennine Mountains, which tower about fifteen thousand feet above the surface. "God was there in a very personal and real way," he said. "First, there was an answer to prayer. I encountered some difficult situations I had never anticipated and just gave up a quick, silent prayer to God. Immediately an answer came—instant communication, no delay. Then there was the guidance God gave us as we explored the surface—particularly the finding of the white rock. We were told by scientists to look for a light-colored rock which would represent the mountains of the moon, the oldest material there. We never dreamed we would find it so easily. Most of the rocks on the moon were covered with dust, but not the white rock. At the base of one of those mountains, at the rim of a small crater, on a pedestal, sat the white rock, almost free from dust. We realized that this was the rock we had come all the way to the moon to find. Sitting there so prominently, it seemed to be saying, 'Here I am. Take me.' "

As he indicates in his book, *To Rule the Night,* Jim was so taken by the beauty of the moon that he was moved to quote a passage from Psalm 121: "I will lift up mine eyes unto the hills, from whence cometh my help." Appropriately a later verse in that chapter reads, "The sun shall not smite thee by day, nor the moon by night."

At the end of his television presentation, he put his experiences in space into perspective. "This evening I speak to you as a man who has studied the heavens, followed the stars, reached the moon," he said. "Then I returned to the earth to tell you that the most important thing that ever happened in my life was finding the rock of Jesus Christ. Won't you invite that Rock into your life?"

144

After taping, as Irwin changed from his spacesuit back into his street clothes, I spent most of my time in the restroom. I had arranged to finish our interview in a car that would be driving him to the Philadelphia airport, but I was feeling so weak and nauseous that I wasn't sure I would make the entire trip. I finally decided to tell Jim about my problem, and I mentioned that I might be hanging my head out the window during part of the drive. I half-expected him to lecture me on the evils of spreading germs and then firmly suggest that it would be better for me *not* to ride with him. But instead, he was quite solicitous. Looking at me with concern, he wondered if there was anything he could do to relieve my discomfort. As we reached the car, he invited me to sit with him in the back seat, and he helped me roll the window down so the breeze would clear my head.

"Let me just ask you a couple of questions," I mumbled. "Do you have any doubts now that you've come back to earth, doubts about God—or was your experience so intense that doubts don't bother you?"

"It was a new level of a relationship [with God]," he replied, looking at me tentatively. "I don't think I'd ever doubt the existence of God or Jesus Christ, but sometimes I wonder why He's working the way He is, or as slow as He is. I'm more perceptive now about the way He's working. I'm closer to Him . . ."

"Do you have more of a sense of the power of the Holy Spirit working in you?"

"Yeah," he replied. "My biggest problem is trying to keep things under control. I was driving so hard and I'd like to do more, but with my heart attack, there's just so much a person can do."

That was the first time he had mentioned the heart attack he had suffered while playing handball after he returned from the space flight. One of the men on the front seat, who was about Jim's age, turned around and asked curiously, "How old are you now?"

"I'm forty-five," he said.

"How about when you had the heart attack?"

"I was forty-three when I had the heart attack, and I had to take it slow. In fact, I was scheduled to go up to a retreat at a high altitude and I wondered if it was all right to go up to nine thousand feet. I eat differently and live differently now. "

"You're still on the road constantly," I observed. "It must be wearing on you."

"It is, but when I get back into the sky, in an airplane, it's a time to rejuvenate." The drive to the airport seemed particularly rough, and Jim, apparently concerned about my well-being, said to the driver, "What have you got back there in your trunk? This is really a bumpy ride." He was glancing at me as he talked, and I imagine I must have been turning completely green.

"I think this car doesn't have shock absorbers," the driver replied.

"I need some air," I said, rolling the window down still farther.

"Sorry for the rough ride, Bill," the driver apologized. "I know this isn't helping your situation."

I could see the airport arrival entrance coming up ahead, and I turned to Jim and said, "There are some other things I'd like to discuss, but I don't think I'm going to be in any shape to talk to you at the airport. I'm sorry about this."

"That's okay, I understand," he said warmly. "I'm just sorry we have to leave you to catch this flight." The efficient, hard-working astronaut who had become so impatient in the TV studio, seemed to have become a genuinely compassionate friend.

As I lay sick in bed at home that night, listening to the strains of the Christmas carols sung by guests in our living room, I wished I'd been able to talk to Jim Irwin more, to know him better. But then I realized his gentle concern for a sick stranger—so different from his usual tough, businesslike manner—probably said more about him than any answers he could have given me.

# *Conclusion*

## TRAIL'S END, TRAIL'S BEGINNING

The spiritual adventures of these celebrities speak eloquently for themselves, so it's probably unwise to try to generalize about them. In fact, as I write this final chapter, the words of the Apostle Paul in 1 Corinthians 1:20 seem to be haunting me: ". . . Where is the scribe? Where is the debater of this age? Has not God made foolish the wisdom of the world?"

But even though my better judgment tells me to leave well enough alone, I sense that some general observations, no matter how inadequate, may be helpful to readers who have set out on the trail of God. There are several themes in the experiences of these celebrities that indicate the variety of means God uses to appeal to individuals with widely divergent personalities and personal backgrounds. One such thread is what might be called the *decision/revelation theme.* Some extremely rational, relatively unemotional people, like Charles Colson and Senator Mark Hatfield, have defined their Christian commitments primarily as decisions, or acts of the will. They saw what had to be done or affirmed, and they did it, with little or no emotional display. David Nelson, on the other hand, tried this rational method up to a point but he needed a shove—a special revelation. So when the right thought about just accepting Christ came into David's mind in that German church, the altar was illuminated by sun streaming through the stained-glass windows. His reaction was to laugh exuberantly at God's response

147

to him. Graham and Treena Kerr experienced similar kinds of revelations—Treena with her vision of Christ, and Graham by having the word "Jesus" placed in his mouth by God.

Another thread that emerges in these accounts might be called the *time theme*. Some people, like Treena Kerr, experienced a definite, point-in-time conversion, similar to the one that gripped the Apostle Paul on the road to Damascus (Acts 9). Carol Lawrence, on the other hand, told me she had no special "moment of truth," but, rather, found that her commitment intensified over a period of time. Even though Carol can't point to one moment as decisive in her faith, she, like those with more dramatic crises, stresses the importance of a life that is unequivocally obedient to Christ.

Perhaps the most fundamental theme of all is the *renewal/ conversion theme*. Some of these Christians, like Pat Boone, Carol Lawrence, Mark Hatfield, James Irwin, and Ruth Carter Stapleton, insisted that their key experience as adults was a renewal of an earlier childhood commitment. Others—Noel Paul Stookey, Graham and Treena Kerr, Dennis Ralston, and David Nelson—described their experiences as a first-time commitment.

I'm convinced that it really doesn't matter which type of experience a person has had or how he describes it, as long as his life involves a total, unequivocal commitment to follow Jesus Christ and find God's will for his life. I've known some people who get worried because they can't point to a specific, Damascus Road conversion. They may even feel somewhat inferior because their conversion wasn't as dramatic as another person's. I myself can't imagine Christ being more concerned with the form or style, than with the continuing quality of a commitment to Him.

A life in Christ hasn't by any means removed all the problems of these celebrities, just as it doesn't immediately eliminate the trials of lesser-known believers. I've attempted to present these famous people, warts and all, because they were open and honest and seemed to want their message to be conveyed in that context. In these pages we've seen them face broken marriages, breakdowns, adulteries, career doubts—almost the entire gamut of human frailties. But the important thing is that their faith has given them tremendous spiritual resources, powerful divine tools to cope with life.

For those who may be interested in embarking on a similar spiritual journey, the experiences of these celebrities suggest that two factors are especially important in getting started. First of all, most of these individuals listened closely to the *witness of other Christians*. Charles Colson was influenced by Tom Phillips; I was especially impressed when he declared Phillips was the only person in his life who had told him it was possible to have a personal relationship with God. Pat Boone was guided to his renewal, or "baptism of the Spirit," by several Christian friends. Treena Kerr found Christ through the urging of her maid, Ruth Turner; Treena, in turn, influenced her husband, Graham, through the witness of a changed life. Dennis Ralston listened to fellow tennis star Stan Smith's description of the Christian life, and he was also encouraged decisively by his wife, Linda.

This tradition of the Christian witness began with Jesus' Great Commission (Matthew 28:19–20) and has been a key factor in this country since Christianity was introduced here. I recall doing a study at Harvard on why the great American evangelist Jonathan Edwards was so successful in helping to spark the Great Awakening in Massachusetts in the 1730s. On the surface, Edwards had nothing going for him. He was an unimpressive speaker and employed no flamboyant gestures or oratorical flourishes. Most of his sermons—with the exception of "Sinners in the Hands of an Angry God"—read like dry theological treatises. Yet emotions ran high during his services, and many were converted.

Why did his preaching have such an impact? I believe the Spirit of God was the cause of the conversions, but the channel through which the Spirit worked was apparently the witness, in one-to-one spiritual discussions, of individual Christians (see Merrill Jensen, ed., *English Historical Documents,* New York, Oxford University Press, 1955, vol. IX, p. 538).

In addition to paying close attention to the words of practicing Christians, it also seems essential that those who want to find God must get involved in a *serious, diligent search for Him.* James urges in his epistle (James 4:8), "Draw near to God and he will draw near to you." That's exactly the approach that Noel Paul Stookey took, as he moved from deep thinking about truth and love to serious discussions with Bob Dylan, with a Christian disk jockey, and with teenager Steve Hance. Stookey *wanted* to find the truth, and he finally did—in Jesus Christ.

Once you as a serious seeker embark on your spiritual quest, you'll ultimately be confronted—as were those in this book—with a series of steps which can lead directly to a secure and powerful relationship with God.

First of all, *you'll recognize that you're separated from God, and you'll have to decide you want to overcome that separation.* In the Bible, this separation is often equated with "sin," and the decision that you want to end the separation may be termed "repentance." (See Ephesians 2:12; Luke 13:1–5; Romans 3:23, 6:23; 1 John 1:8–9, 3:4–10).

Secondly, as you turn away from your separation from God, you'll move into a *total commitment of your life to the God who was incarnated in Jesus Christ.* (See Luke 14:25–33; Revelation 3:20; John 1:12). This step involves putting God first, and everything and everyone else second. It involves a decision to follow Christ unequivocally, just as His disciples did (though some faltered on occasion). Another way of describing this step is that you'll ask God, as He revealed Himself in Christ, to take over your life.

This second step in becoming a Christian also involves affirming certain historic beliefs, like the resurrection of Jesus, and making public your acceptance of Jesus as Lord (Romans 10:9–10).

The third and final step in becoming a Christian is *to live a life which is obedient to Christ and which bears the fruits of His Spirit.* Submission to God is essential to achieve this Spirit-oriented life-style. The reborn Christian seeks God's will through prayer, Bible study, and the advice of other Christians. Then, after he learns God's will, he obeys it. The Bible tells us that the Christian who is empowered by the Spirit will find that his faith leads to good works (James 2:17), and that the "fruit of the Spirit"—such as love, joy, peace, patience, and kindness—abounds in his relationships with others (Galatians 5:22–23).

I could see this fruit of the Spirit in the lives of many of these well-known Christians whom I visited. And I found my own faith being strengthened and the horizons of my relationship with Christ expanding and becoming more beautiful. Genuine Christians on every social, economic, and denominational level can establish an immediate bond as spiritual brothers and sisters, and begin to learn from one another and enjoy the common Spirit. From the best-known film and stage stars, to the leading politicians, to every ordinary and unknown lay person, we are all one, all servants as well as children of the King.